THE PARISH NURSE

THE PARISH NURSE

Providing a Minister of Health
for Your Congregation

Granger E. Westberg

with Jill Westberg McNamara

Augsburg • Minneapolis

THE PARISH NURSE
Providing a Minister of Health for Your Congregation

Scripture quotations unless otherwise noted are from the Holy Bible: New International Version. Copyright © 1978 by the New York International Bible Society. Used by permission of Zondervan Bible Publishers.

The term, Parish Nurse, is a registered service mark of Lutheran General Health Care System, Park Ridge, IL. Used by permission.

Material from Lutheran General Hospital is copyright © by Lutheran General Hospital, Park Ridge, Illinois, and is used by permission.

Material adapted from *Nurses in Churches: A Manual for Developing Parish Nurse Services and Networks* by Jan Striepe is copyright © 1989 by Jan Striepe and is used by permission of the author.

Material from Iowa Lutheran Hospital's Minister of Health and Education Program is copyright © 1990 by David F. Carlson and is used by permission.

Chapter six is based on the experience of Joan E. Linden.

Cover design: Pollock Design Group

Library of Congress Cataloging-in-Publication Data

Westberg, Granger E.
    The parish nurse : providing a minister of health for your
  congregation / Granger E. Westberg with Jill Westberg McNamara.
    p.   cm.
  ISBN 0-8066-2458-2 (alk. paper)
  1. Pastoral medicine. 2. Nursing—Religious aspects—
Christianity. I. McNamara, Jill Westberg. II. Title.
BV4335.W45 1990
610.73'43—dc20   90-43206
                                      CIP

Manufactured in the U.S.A.   AF 9-2458

99 98 97 96 95 2 3 4 5 6 7 8 9 10

Contents

1

Why a Parish Nurse Program?

This book was written for lay people and pastors who have long cherished the hope that their congregations might provide a wholistic health ministry for their parishioners as well as other people in their neighborhoods. I will describe an action-research project that places nurses on the staffs of congregations as ministers of health, working alongside pastors and others who are dedicated to wholistic ministry.

As recently as a hundred years ago, Christian churches were leaders in the health field, building the finest hospitals the world has ever known and educating thousands of religiously motivated women as nurses. Today, scientific medicine, aware of its limitations, is looking for assistance in preventive medicine, in health education, and in helping to motivate people to care for their own health.

In our day there is a great interest in health and whole- person theology. The media bombard us daily with stories about nutrition, stress management, self-care, exercise, and preventive medicine. Many articles have been written about the interrelationship of body, mind, and spirit. Clearly people are interested in these things or we would not hear so much about them. However, applying the wisdom of popular magazine articles to our lives has its problems. Even if their advice has merit, we probably will not succeed. Most of the time we need outside support to find the courage to change our life-styles. But we do not always know where to find such help. Although most of us really do want to bring about some beneficial changes in our lives, we may never quite get around to doing so. How do we get the necessary motivation to change our unhealthy habits? And what does all of this have to do with religion?

Personal motivation for a serious life change has its roots in one's outlook on life. I am, of course, referring to a person's philosophy of life, belief system, or faith stance. This brings us into the realm of religion. The central concern of the Christian faith has to do with how people view the nature and destiny of the human being. Followers of Jesus Christ hold his outlook on life in high regard. His worldview—even his cosmic view—and his concept of the kinds of relationships that can take place between human beings and the Creator give meaning to our lives. Such an outlook on life is one of the major characteristics of a truly healthy person.

Our faith motivates us to examine ourselves and to ask ourselves some serious questions: Why are you so dissatisfied with your present life-style that you want to change it? Do you sense that there is more to life than you are now experiencing?

Few people go out of their way to seek preventive health care—and they are almost never willing to pay for it. Doctors know how difficult it is to motivate people to change unhealthy life-styles. Physicians, in any discussion with clergy, invariably ask, "How can we motivate our patients to want to change their unhealthy life-styles?" During the few minutes in which doctors see patients in the examination room, there is little opportunity to motivate major life changes.

This is where the church comes in. If motivation is intimately tied up with how people look at life, it follows that its energy would be heightened when people are in the company of those who also believe that such motivation comes through spiritual commitment. The church does such motivating of people on a weekly basis and continues to care about people throughout their entire lives. A parish nurse who does her work within the context of a community of faith might offer just that kind of needed inspiration.*

Care for all of the people of God is a part of the church's mission, of its understanding of the Christian gospel. We are talking here about care for the whole person—body, mind, and spirit. The Bible has much to say about the importance of the interrelationship of body and soul. The New Testament tells us that Jesus, when he sent out his disciples, told them not only to preach the kingdom of God, but also to heal the sick (Luke 9:2).

Much of what happens in churches throughout the country is just the sort of thing that helps people stay well: regular opportunities for building friendships; help through prayer, music, and worship; opportunities to serve and, in turn, be served by

---

*Because all of our present parish nurses are women, we will use feminine pronouns. We hope male nurses will join our ranks soon.

others. All of these help create an attitude of gratitude and hope and are known to contribute to a person's total health.

This approach is in total sympathy with the wholistic health movement, which takes seriously a person's belief system. If that system is faulty, it can affect the way in which the body functions. If wholistic concepts are integrated with one's religious beliefs, each will motivate the other. And at this moment in history, the church is sorely needed to help motivate people to put body, mind, and spirit together, and to convince them that the integration of all three can lead to true health and wholeness.

The whole-person approach to health is remarkably congruent with a full, well-rounded life. At a time when many congregations feel they are stagnating, spending too much time talking about God and too little making the Word come alive in action, perhaps they should reexamine that most fundamental Christian concept, salvation, and remember that it means "being made whole." The time has come for the church to resume its concern with health care and to once again pick up the reins of innovation and leadership in the crucial and sometimes forgotten area of ministry.

Throughout this book and particularly in chapter 5, I will describe what parish nurses do. At this point, however, I want to identify the five primary areas to which most of these nurses devote their time and energy. Parish nurses serve first of all as health educators, planning and organizing seminars, workshops, and classes on a wide range of health and wellness topics. They also are personal health counselors, meeting with church members to talk over health problems and questions. Parish nurses are teachers of volunteers, identifying and training lay people to serve as visitors, leaders of programs, and volunteers in a variety of capacities. Parish nurses serve as liaisons with community health organizations, acting as gatekeepers, opening doors to many types of health care for those needing such care. They also are clarifiers of the close relationship between faith and health, talking with church members about the deeper issues of life related to their health.

This book grows out of testing the parish nurse model in all kinds of churches and in many different situations throughout the United States: Tucson, Arizona; Sioux City, Spencer, and Des Moines, Iowa; San Jose, California; Minneapolis, Minnesota; and Chicago, Illinois. In each place, there are variations in the way the program is organized. Each congregation is free to structure the program as best suits its needs. Much depends on the personality of the congregation, its location, and the kind of people who attend that church. Much also depends on the particular gifts of the nurse who accepts the challenge of this pioneering assignment.

Two-thirds of the churches in this study have volunteer programs in which nurses give from four to ten hours per week. Then, as members of the congregation begin to experience the program's value, as well as its value for others in the community who may not be related to the church, they appropriate funds in the annual budget to pay the nurses.

Most of the churches in the other one-third have salaried nurses who serve half-time, or approximately 20 hours per week. Those nurses are a vital part of the church staff, reporting directly to the pastor. An attempt is made to compensate them at the rate established by local hospitals.

Our primary finding in this experimental project, begun in 1983, is that there are nurses throughout

America who have been dreaming of the day when they could combine their medical training and their philosophical concerns. Despite the shortage of nurses, we had no difficulty throughout the several years of this experimental project in finding unusually qualified women with exceptional spiritual maturity. Their ability to move easily into many different kinds of caring situations within the congregation convinced many church members that the parish nurse's talents add a much needed dimension to the local church's ministry.

Many women who have gone into nursing were motivated by a desire to serve people in a whole-person manner. Many have been disappointed by positions in hospitals or clinics where there was no time for the kind of personal caring they felt patients needed so desperately. Complete freedom to minister wholistically to patients is the gift that parish nurse positions offer these women.

Our second finding during these start-up years was that interest in parish nurses is not limited to any particular group in society. While the first six nurses, sponsored by Lutheran General Hospital in Park Ridge, Illinois, were all located in large suburban churches, the next group worked in congregations in the lowest income neighborhoods of inner-city Chicago. At the same time, there was sudden, amazing growth in the rural areas and smaller towns of Iowa. Shortly thereafter, more than 20 congregations in California's Silicon Valley sent us enthusiastic reports.

Our third finding was that Catholic and Protestant churches work extremely well together in an undertaking of this kind.

Our fourth finding was that community hospitals, religious or secular, have a particular interest in this model of health care as they set about changing their image as institutions that provide services only to the sick. The many hospitals that sponsor programs in one way or another see the parish nurse as a link with the local community.

A growing number of churches are intentionally becoming centers to which people can turn for health care with a spiritual dimension. These congregations ask how they can help bring about a climate that promotes wholistic living. The parish nurse project is the creation of lay people and clergy who are determined to follow Christ's command to heal as well as to teach and preach. They believe that such a combined ministry can be carried out in local congregations. How such healing or caring aspects of the church's ministry will develop remains to be seen. But those parish nurses who are already involved in this ministry constantly discover new ways of bringing body and soul together. Our experience with the several hundred churches that have parish nurses on their staffs convinces us that such nurses can work wonders in helping to clarify the interrelationship between faith and good health.

Currently, a national organization of parish nurses is being formed. The group will set goals and standards for the profession, as well as develop a manual of information for interested church councils, pastors, and lay leaders. Information on new developments can be obtained from the National Parish Nurse Resource Center, Lutheran General Hospital, 1775 West Dempster Street, Park Ridge, IL 60068.

2

A Brief History of the Parish Nurse Program

If a pollster were to knock on the door of homes in almost any community throughout the United States and ask, "What are the health agencies in this community?" what would the answer be? Most people would give the name of a local hospital and perhaps some well-known medical clinic in the area. People generally equate health care with hospitals and doctors.

But today the word *health* is taking on characteristics related to more than just "sickness care." It is not enough to mention only hospitals and doctors who generally spend most of their time taking care of people only after they become sick.

Nurses have long been concerned about this overemphasis on sickness care. Many have moved out into the community, away from hospitals, seeking to find ways of preventing people from becoming ill. They have frequently expressed the belief that perhaps one-third of the patients they have seen in hospitals over the past 50 years would not have become that ill if someone in the community had been sensitive to their earlier cries for help. And if they had received care earlier, their symptoms would have been reversible.

As a pastor I have had an unusually close relationship with the nursing profession. I started my career as a parish pastor in the university community of Bloomington, Illinois, and chanced to spend a week as chaplain in a large Chicago hospital. I lived with residents and interns. I got less sleep and drank more coffee than during any other week of my life as the doctors and nurses involved me in every conceivable human situation.

That one week changed my life. Three years later I became the first full-time chaplain of that hospital and, at age 30, the first chaplain under 70 years of age. For eight years I taught several hours each week in that hospital's school of nursing, and we developed the case study method of teaching the relationship between religion and health.

Then, out of the blue, came a call to a joint professorship in Religion and Health at the University of Chicago Medical School and Divinity School. We soon inaugurated a weekly religion-medicine case conference over a brown bag lunch. At each conference the problem of a current patient was presented by the patient's attending physician and resident, a nurse who knew the patient well, and one of the hospital chaplains who had ministered to the patient. This triumvirate of doctor, nurse, and pastor symbolized for me a type of patient care I had always dreamed about. The conferences were attended by students in nursing, medicine, and theology. There were usually from 10 to 30 people present. The intent of each conference was to take a serious look at the spiritual dimensions of the patient's illness and to begin the necessary dialogue among these three professions—disciplines that had so much in common. Some doctors left the conference scratching their heads and saying, "How did they get me involved in this unscientific approach to illness?" But others said, "This is the first time I have ever even thought about the religious dimension of my patients' illnesses. And it's the first time I've ever sat down on an equal footing with nurses and pastors and had to slug it out with them!" And the nurses said, "This is what ought to happen every day on the hospital floors." They kept urging me to expand the concept.

The religion-medicine case conference convinced a number of people that illness is a multidimensional phenomenon and that fragmentation of the patient is one of our greatest problems.

During my 12 years in the highly structured setting of a teaching and research hospital where we saw only very sick people, I began to think about the one-third of those patients who, according to many nurses, would never have become so ill if their symptoms had been detected much sooner.

Nurses convinced me that the field of preventive medicine would never go anywhere if it remained only in the hands of physicians. People in other professions and with other skills were needed, including parish clergy who see people on a regular basis and often in informal settings.

Eventually I moved to the Department of Preventive Medicine, University of Illinois College of Medicine. With the encouragement and financial support of the W. K. Kellogg Foundation, we eventually set up a dozen experimental family doctors' offices in church buildings. In these settings, teams comprised of doctor, nurse, and pastor cared for patients, using a joint approach. These wholistic health centers became teaching centers for literally hundreds of physicians, nurses, and pastors from all over the United States and Canada, as well as a number from abroad. The evaluation of the project by outside observers suggests that they hope we will continue to operate these nonprofit doctors' offices as demonstration projects. They were particularly impressed with the openness of the several staffs to creative ways of dealing with the whole patient. They saw the nurses as catalysts in getting representatives of medicine and theology to talk with each other. Nurses seemed to have one foot in the humanities and one foot in the sciences and thereby were able to bridge the unnecessary gap between these two very old and esteemed professions.

We have expanded this wholistic concept into hundreds of congregations throughout the United States and Canada. The specific work of the nurses varies according to the setting of a given church. The primary thrust of the nurses' work is to identify early cries for help and to intervene before problems require hospitalization. The nurses, therefore, are doing most of their work in the areas of prevention and wellness. Through seminars, workshops, discussion groups, and Sunday school classes, they help individuals understand that health care is part of the responsible stewardship of one's life. With this in mind, it is the role of the nurse to involve people in their own health care and in the care of their neighbors. As people work together toward good health, each individual's load is lightened.

When I discussed the parish nurse project with a number of pastors, they showed greater interest in the concept than I had expected. Pastors spend much of their time calling on sick parishioners and often feel frustrated by their inability to deal with the problems of these patients in a more wholistic manner. They say, "Perhaps we could team up in some kind of total patient care and bring about results that we are not seeing now." One pastor said: "I feel all alone in ministering to some of these difficult people. I can seldom get doctors to discuss problems, but I've always had excellent relationships with nurses in my hospital calling. Perhaps putting such a nurse on our staff would be a good step for our congregation to take."

Nurses have been serving people with a spirit of caring, touching them and talking with them. That is exactly what is needed in every congregation—a balance between touching and talking, or communicating. Without the touch the talk does not carry much power.

Clergy are now more open to ideas related to health and wholeness because everything they have tried to say about the value of living a healthy, balanced life is now being verified and clarified by current research in the health sciences. A nurse on the church staff as a representative of the health sciences is a visible symbol of the close tie between one's faith and one's health.

It is, of course, still unusual to have a nurse's office in a church building. But this is a way of giving people easy access to a qualified health provider. People who just happen to be walking by are free to drop in and talk about anything on their hearts. Often they want to talk about physical problems that are not all that urgent but that make it natural to move on to the greater human problems that may be causing the physical ones. When a nurse senses that a person has medical problems that need a doctor's attention, her encouragement may cause that person to see a doctor sooner than that person would have otherwise. A good parish nurse takes time to listen, to counsel, to pray with people, and to introduce them to small support groups. She represents an exciting new development for ministry in the congregation.

But let us return for a moment to the question with which we began: What are the health agencies in our communities? If hospitals and doctors spend the major portion of their time with people after they get sick, what institutions in our culture help us to prevent sickness? There are at least five: the home, the school, the church and other voluntary organizations, the workplace, and the public health department. When these five are all in good shape, we are very fortunate. If any one of them is not doing its job, people begin to feel unwell. Healthy churches offer a variety of interest and discussion groups, social activities, music, drama, and ongoing educational opportunities for all ages. The parish nurse can add another vital dimension: preparing the congregation for its role in preventive medicine, helping people to understand the ingredients of a full, rounded life.

Much of what I have said about collaboration between pastor and nurse is drawn from my own experience. Nurses have backed me during my struggles with doctors who could not understand why the hospital should bother to have a chaplain. Nurses knew what I was going through because they themselves had been thwarted so long in their efforts to bring about changes in patient care. They longed to develop creative new methods of teaching and of relating to patients but were told that there was no time for such things. Long before anyone wrote articles on wholeness, wellness, and preventive health care, nurses were already practicing whole-person care, at least for the few moments they were allowed to escape from the technical aspects of their work.

Nurses are national treasures, reservoirs of compassion and strength, and pearls of great price that have been hidden from view for far too long. For more than 40 years nurses have pleaded with the medical profession that it become more oriented toward preventive medicine, that it concentrate on teaching people how to stay well. Now is their chance to reach thousands of people in the informal setting of an institution that is ready to rethink its role in motivating people toward healthy living.

3

Eight Steps to a Parish Nurse Program

This chapter provides the basic procedures for congregations interested in adding a parish nurse as a minister of health to their church staff.

1. Learn All You Can

If you would like to have a parish nurse as a minister of health in your congregation, you will want to get as much background information as you can. If at all possible, meet with nurses, pastors, and lay people who are already involved in such a project. Until more books and articles are written about the parish nurse project, it is my hope that this book will answer many of your questions. Here are a few other suggestions that may help you in this first step.

A. As you read this book, think about the ways its contents would or would not relate to your situation. No two churches are alike and no two nurses are alike. Allow for a great deal of flexibility when styling your health ministry.

B. Share this book with several other people and arrange some times to discuss the parish nurse project.

C. Read articles in newspapers, magazines, and medical and nursing journals dealing with new concepts in preventive medicine and wellness care. The parish nurse program is essentially concerned with how to keep people well.

D. Brainstorm with like-minded friends (include some medical professionals) about how this project might work specifically in your church and in your neighborhood and town. No doubt they will be able to see some additional possibilities as well as stumbling blocks of which you may not be aware. If your friends like the concept, it might help to do an informal assessment of needs to help determine the direction this project should take in your church.

E. Begin to think about the kind of nurse you are looking for, because her abilities will set the pattern for the program. See Step 6 for information about selecting a nurse.

2. The Pastor

Assuming that you are not the pastor of your congregation, it is crucial that you meet with him or her at the beginning of your journey. If the pastor is not interested in the idea, there is little hope for success. Therefore, the presentation of the concept to your pastor is of utmost importance.

Experience has shown that if only one person approaches the pastor, the project may very easily be dismissed as "too difficult to tackle at the present time." But if several members who have thoroughly studied the concept make a special group appointment with the pastor, it will be received as a much more serious proposal. If this group includes a physician, the idea cannot easily be dismissed.

Thus, before you meet with the pastor, you need to find the people who can provide the needed impetus to your efforts. Choose those whom you have found to be receptive to your proposal in earlier conversations and who are highly regarded in the congregation. Perhaps their own work or life experience has demonstrated to them the need for preventive care and concern for the whole person. Try to enlist nurses as advocates for the project. Most congregations have one or two members who are, or have been, active in nursing. In larger churches it often comes as a surprise to discover how many nurses are on the membership roll. In my experience, nurses in the congregation have been the best supporters of the parish nurse project.

When you make your presentation, be sure that you are well prepared to back up your statements with facts from the experience of congregations that currently have parish nurse programs. One person in your group might present the overall picture, and others could address individual concerns. Your pastor may be one of the many who will almost immediately begin to describe situations in which a nurse could be of real assistance.

The pastor who chooses to support the idea now has a key role to play in all future developments. This may include the following:

A. Provide support for the project both in the congregation and in the community at large.

B. Assist in the selection of persons from the congregation to work with an exploratory task force.

C. Help the original group bring the message to the congregation.

D. Help select and contact other pastors in the community who might be interested in a parish nurse project to be conducted jointly by several congregations.

E. Undergird the project with the strong biblical foundation for whole-person health care that is found in both the Old and the New Testaments.

3. The Congregation

It is now time to involve a wider group of people in the process. This is the point at which a task force can be very helpful, particularly if its members represent a cross section of the congregation.

Who should tell the story? Whenever presentations are made to committees in the church, it is important that the presenters have done their homework. Committee members have a right to hear several points of view on a matter they will be asked to support.

You will find yourself telling this story over and over again, not only to the church's various organizations, but also to individuals who have heard something about it but do not have all the facts. Remember, it is a radical idea to suggest that a congregation become involved in health care. Why would a church want to have a nurse on the staff? We have noted earlier the unfortunate reality that for fully a century we have separated health care and spiritual care to such an extent that there has been no real communication between the two. Now is the time for such communication to be resumed.

To bolster your confidence, start with a group that will almost assure your success: nurses. Invite the nurses in your congregation and perhaps other nurses who would be interested to an evening devoted to discussion of the project. In the past, the unanimous response to such invitations has been one of gratitude that at last someone has recognized the potential of nurses in the area of preventive medicine and health education.

After your meeting with the nurses, arrange to make a presentation to the congregation. Do not ignore women's and men's groups. Encourage the members of your task force to be present at coffee hours where they can listen informally to the kinds of questions people are raising.

When the task force and the pastor think the time has come for presenting the proposal to the official church board or council, ask for a full hour to make your presentation. If it is your congregation's policy to present each new proposal to one of several standing committees, then that, of course, is the route to follow.

The meeting with the church board or council usually turns out to be the most difficult presentation of all, because these officially elected people have to fit this new project into the congregation's budget. They probably have a half dozen other proposals clamoring for attention. In other words, expect resistance from board members who may be championing other causes. Remember that this is only natural, and if your project is third or fourth on the list, be content with the reality of a waiting period. However, remember also that the pastor usually knows what proposals are brewing and will be able to suggest the times when yours might fit in well with future plans. Be sure to ask the pastor to help you decide when the presentation should be made.

Even if and when the church board decides in favor of the proposal, be prepared for a necessary lead time of three months to a year. At this point it would be wise to begin organizing a health cabinet or committee.

4. Form a Health Cabinet or Committee

Every church with a parish nurse should have a health cabinet or committee that can become a true support for the nurse and to which she is to report on a regular, perhaps monthly, basis. (See chapter 4 for more information.)

The health cabinet is usually made up of six to twelve people in the congregation who have some interest in the relationship of religion and health. If possible, health cabinets should include a doctor, several nurses, a social worker, a health educator, a school teacher, and other competent, interested people in the congregation.

The pastor is an important ex-officio member of the health cabinet and needs to be present at every meeting. This is of particular importance since the parish nurse serves under the pastor's direction and is considered a vital member of the ministerial staff.

The health cabinet has the following responsibilities:

A. Educating its members about wholistic concepts of health care through regular discussions of recommended books and articles.

B. Assessing the particular kinds of needs in the congregation that the parish nurse might address.

C. Working out the necessary financial and legal arrangements. (See pages 100-103.)

D. Recruiting, interviewing, and selecting the parish nurse.

E. Making the necessary arrangements for the nurse's participation in continuing education on a regular basis, both at home and away.

F. Keeping the congregation informed about the parish nurse's work through regular items in the church's newsletter as well as through reports to the church board or council.

G. Developing opportunities to meet with neighborhood churches and local hospitals to discuss ways of working together, perhaps integrating similar programs.

H. Assisting with health fairs and seminars to which the whole community is invited.

5. An Option: Establishing Links with a Local Hospital

In our experimental model of the parish nurse program in the Chicago area, we found it much to our advantage to have close ties with a hospital. While it is quite possible for a church to support a successful parish nurse project on its own, there are benefits in a hospital relationship that should be seriously considered.

Since the parish nurse's role is new and not yet clearly defined, it may be difficult for her to work in isolation from her professional peers. The relationship with a hospital answers a parish nurse's need for regular collegial support from other nurses.

For example, if there are several churches in the same general area, it would be helpful if a hospital, somewhat central to all of them, be chosen as the weekly or semiweekly meeting place. The hospital might provide for the parish nurses a program of continuing education by allied health professionals who are part of the institution.

It is wise for congregations who are planning a parish nurse project to have an early discussion with people at a local hospital. If there is a department of pastoral care, first talk over the idea with one of the chaplains. Ideally, this department will already have a good relationship with the local churches, and progressive chaplains will quickly grasp the possibilities of the concept.

After your discussion with the chaplains, meet with the hospital's administrator and administrative staff as well as with key members of the hospital's board of directors. You may be dubious about your chances of selling the project to the administrator, but often it is easier than expected. Today a new spirit among hospital administrators places great emphasis on the relationship of the hospital to the local community. Whereas, in the past, hospitals seemed to be concerned chiefly about people who were sick enough to be put to bed, today hospitals see their task much more wholistically. Gradually they are becoming interested in teaching people how to stay well. Hospitals now understand that their future lies in very different areas than in the past. They want to be seen not only as places for treatment of the sick, but also as institutions that place a high priority on "wellness."

The degree of hospital involvement can be negotiated. If the administrator expresses support for the parish nurse concept, be prepared to suggest ways in which the hospital could be involved. Here are three possible levels of involvement:

A. First level: The local hospital would provide a meeting room for a small number of parish nurses who would come together for approximately three hours once or twice a week.

The main reason for meeting in a hospital rather than in one of the churches is to develop a relationship with its medical staff, particularly the nurses. The hospital would be asked to provide a nurse educator as the coordinator of these meetings. This educator would listen to the kinds of questions the parish nurses ask and then invite appropriate professionals from the hospital's staff to address issues in their area of expertise. Such an arrangement would provide vital backup in these early stages of this new direction in nursing.

B. Second level: This level would include everything in the first level plus a close working relationship with the hospital's chaplaincy department. On this working level, a chaplain would act as coordinator with the nurse educator. This would assure that a theologically trained person would attend the regular meetings and discuss with the parish nurses the many new concerns raised when attempting to integrate the physical and spiritual dimensions of illness and health. If the hospital has no pastoral care department, clergy in the community who have been clinically trained in hospital work and counseling could act as coordinators.

C. Third level: The local hospital initiates a parish nurse program in the geographical area it serves. In this case, the hospital selects someone to coordinate the project who is responsible for locating from three to six churches and discussing with them the feasibility of having nurses on their church staffs. If such an extensive involvement of the hospital with the church appeals to your congregation, you may find more information about such an arrangement on pages 104-132 (Iowa Lutheran Hospital and Lutheran General Hospital).

6. Select the Parish Nurse

Your pastor and the health cabinet will bear chief responsibility for selection of the parish nurse. You will need to find a way to screen each candidate's medical qualifications. This can be done through your local hospital or by a physician who has agreed to serve as a backup for the nurse.

The basic requirement is that your minister of health be a registered nurse who, if possible, has a baccalaureate degree (see pages 91-92). From that point on much depends on the human and spiritual quality of this person—her ability to relate warmly to all kinds of people and to relate what she has learned from previous professional jobs. Public health, school nursing, and psychiatric nursing are helpful backgrounds, but several of our successful parish nurses have had medical-surgical, oncological, or pediatric experience. Who the person is takes precedence over the specifics of her job experience or education.

The qualifications for a parish nurse depend on the job description developed by the health cabinet. Generally, parish nurses do not give "hands on" care. If there are physicians nearby, it is best to refer people with strictly medical needs to a physician. However, in a rural area where the nearest doctor may be twenty or more miles away, we suggest the selection of a parish nurse who is a nurse practitioner (a registered nurse with advanced training enabling her to provide primary care services).

There are various sources through which you can recruit your nurse. These might include placing a story in your church newsletter or advertisements in the local papers as well as in nursing journals. If you are working in conjunction with a local hospital, the hospital could recruit through its own channels.

Does the parish nurse have to be a member of the congregation? Our experience persuades us that it does not matter. Sometimes the nurse is an active member; sometimes she belongs to another church. In other situations, Protestant congregations have chosen Roman Catholic nurses and have been pleased with their choices.

We have learned that the parish nurse needs to have a great deal of visibility. Because of the quiet nature of her work, people need to be reminded of her presence and availability. She should be at church every Sunday morning, participating from time to time in the reading of Scripture at worship services and making announcements related to the health ministry. She needs to be included in educational programs and be part of such informal events as fellowship hours with refreshments. With such visibility, it becomes easy and natural for members to talk with her. This often leads to further appointments.

The nurse you choose will need to be quietly assertive and will have to make herself known in many different ways during the early years of this project so that people understand what she can do for them. As the parish nurse program is currently structured, the nurse's main objectives are to help people assume responsibility for their own health and to help them grasp new insights about the many causes of illness. This entails considerable teaching and the development of various support groups. It is the responsibility of the parish nurse to create interest in a variety of health-related programs.

The parish nurse must be a sensitive listener so that people will feel comfortable in her presence and know that she cares about their needs. As she listens, she will pick up signals about what it is they are really trying to express. It is crucial that the nurse you select has a talent for counseling. Such skills can be improved by attending workshops or training programs.

Your parish nurse should also be skilled in recruiting and training volunteers who can then assist her in many different ways. Not the least of their contributions may be information about persons in the congregation who are going through difficulties that can trigger illness.

The most important qualification of the parish nurse is a high degree of spiritual maturity. In our interviews with a large number of candidates, we were pleased, though not surprised, to note that most of them could articulate their Christian faith in a manner that was quiet but effective. Such maturity is essential in the building of this unique program, set in the context of a worshiping and serving congregation. The parish nurse will frequently find herself in situations where a religiously focused comment or a spoken prayer may be more valuable to the worried parishioner who has come to her for help than immediate attention to physical symptoms. If the nurse is able to discuss concepts of faith with persons who are raising questions concerning their personal value systems, she will be even more helpful.

In secular work situations, nurses are not expected to deal with the spiritual problems of the people they serve. Parish nurses, however, are encouraged to move into the area of caring because they know that illness has a dimension beyond the realm of science, a dimension that has been neglected to the detriment of both patient and nurse.

Parish nurses must be highly competent medically, but they should also be willing to be challenged intellectually through books and discussions about practical theological issues.

7. Continuing Education for the Parish Nurse

Your parish nurse should attend some kind of educational program so that she will be better prepared to meet the demands of her unique position.

Because the parish nurse program is still so new, I am unable to suggest much in the way of specific educational opportunities. However, educational programs are becoming available in various parts of the country. Furthermore, most large hospitals offer continuing education courses for nurses, and parish nurses should be expected to keep up with the medical and scientific side of their profession.

As noted earlier, when several nurses live and work in the same town or general area, it is ideal for them to meet regularly. In this way they can offer one another mutual support in their unique responsibilities and have medical experts sit with them to discuss the medical and nursing aspects of their work. Parish nurses must deal with problems that nurses in other specialties may not encounter. These include, especially, the spiritual dimensions of illness. Because of this, it would be useful to ask a chaplain or knowledgeable parish pastor to sit in with the group on a continuing basis.

Because such an arrangement may not be possible, I suggest another idea. A growing number of hospitals with chaplaincy departments offer courses in pastoral care and counseling for local clergy. Pastors are pleased when nurses participate in these seminars because so many of the pastoral problems under discussion have a physical or psychological component. Clergy know that nurses make valuable contributions to discussions of the patients' spiritual needs. Nurses are well acquainted with both medicine and the humanities. Because of this, they are natural catalysts who facilitate communication between theology and medicine.

Also available at some hospitals are courses in clinical pastoral education (CPE) that meet on a weekly basis over a period of six to nine months. Such courses are ideal opportunities, for they provide the parish nurse with all the clinical material and knowledge she needs in her own church setting. In this type of clinical pastoral education, the questions of body and soul are constantly raised, and these are precisely the kinds of issues the parish nurse faces on an almost daily basis. The Parish Nurse Resource Center in Illinois (address on page 140) is prepared to offer guidance to congregations wishing to provide continuing education for their parish nurses.

8. The New Parish Nurse

The first few weeks are spent in introducing the parish nurse to the congregation and helping the members understand what her role will be in that church's ministry.

Soon after the parish nurse's arrival, the church should have a worship service or special gathering to introduce her and to explore the congregation's role in the health ministry of the church. A sermon by the pastor and brief presentations by members of the health cabinet could explain the underlying reasons for this new ministry. Then the new parish nurse could be formally introduced to the people, and she could respond with a statement of her own understanding of her ministry. Such a special event is essential if the program is to get off to a good start. The congregation must see the program from the beginning as an integral part of its whole-person ministry.

The following are some of the important things the new parish nurse can do during her first weeks on the job:

A. Get settled in her office. It should be easily accessible to everyone, including those who use wheelchairs. It should, of course, be equipped with a telephone. It should offer privacy to those who come to speak with her.

B. Spend considerable time with the pastor and church staff, exploring ways in which the program can connect with the other programs of the church. Staff members should have the opportunity for considerable input, since they usually have their fingers on the congregation's pulse.

C. Arrange frequent meetings with the health cabinet during the first several months so that its members can become acquainted with the new parish nurse and with each other. During these early weeks, the nurse will have many questions.

D. Meet with the chairpersons of the congregation's various standing committees. Only as these leaders become acquainted with the new parish nurse and learn of her interests and abilities will they be able to use her talents effectively.

E. Have blood pressure checks after several Sunday services. This provides an excellent way for people to meet with the nurse and to decide whether they would like to have further conversations with her.

F. Be available for meetings with small groups to discuss subjects of their choosing that are related to the areas of the nurse's competence.

G. Begin to develop a file of the congregation's shut-in and elderly members so that the nurse may visit them and make an assessment of their needs. Although it is not her role to be a home health nurse, she will, nevertheless, then be in a position to ascertain whether church volunteers could assist such persons.

H. Survey the congregation to find out where the members' needs lie. Such a survey will also help the parish nurse discover what skills are available within the membership and which people might be willing to volunteer their services.

4

The Health Cabinet

Many Americans are kept well, at least in part, by their relationship with their community of faith. Caring for one another is a natural dynamic in most churches, synagogues, and other centers of faith. Health cabinets (often called health and wellness committees) were designed for the express purpose of helping congregations enhance their ministries of health. A congregation interested in adding a parish nurse to its staff is encouraged to form a health cabinet early in the planning process.

The Christian perspective of health includes our whole lives. Health of body, mind, and spirit is viewed as a gift to nurture and to employ. However, in Western society our thinking is often disease oriented, with health defined as the absence of disease. This negative approach stresses fear and a moving away from illness, rather than a reaching out to good health. Even preventive medicine is often accepted out of a sense of fear. Too often we take care of ourselves more out of a wish to avoid illness than out of a desire to maintain good health. We believe that as long as we don't get sick, we are healthy.

In the Christian tradition, health is seen as an ongoing process. Good health is not an end in itself, but rather it is an enabler. It gives us the energy and vitality to serve and love others, and thus good health is seen in the context of purpose. It is a liberator. With this Christian perspective, we have a good foundation for health promotion, not just disease prevention.

If we were to examine churches throughout the country, what would we find them doing in the area of health care? We would probably find that most congregations do well in crisis care. If someone becomes sick, people rally around to support that individual. They bring meals, help clean the house, take care of the children, or do whatever else they can to help. Even persons unrelated to the church know that if a crisis is preventing them from buying food for their family, a local church may be willing to help them.

Education is another area in which churches function well. In many churches, courses on health-related subjects are taught to people of all ages. Creative stress management, the handling of grief and loss, and training in cardiopulmonary resuscitation (CPR) are all popular topics.

However, the potential for a health ministry goes well beyond crisis care and education. The role of a health cabinet is to help church communities reach people before they are in crisis so that problems can be reversed before professional attention is required. The educational programs already in existence are part of the answer, but the health cabinet will come up with new ways to reach people—especially those who do not attend the courses.

The church has many advantages as a healing institution. It welcomes people of all ages. It welcomes many family configurations, and our families provide the main health support system for most of us. To have an institution that nourishes such a support system is invaluable. We come to church together as a family—a family that includes single-parent families and single people. In other areas of our lives, children go off to school and parents go off to work. Or the mother goes to one activity, the father to something else, and the children to yet another activity. The one place where we can come together as a family is the church.

The church is a powerful influence on our lives. It is one of the few places where it is acceptable to talk about and examine our values and our life-styles and see whether they are in conflict or in harmony with each other.

In the church we are accepted both in sickness and in health. We don't need a pain for our ticket of admission, yet we are still accepted if we do get sick. One of the great advantages of this relationship is that when we do become ill, we are surrounded by people who have known us in health. They know our strengths even though those strengths may now be hidden because we are consumed by illness. They are able to call forth in us those strengths that can help us overcome our illness.

Many congregations have asked: "What can we do to further the health ministry in our church? We don't have the space, the money, or the energy to start a health center, but we still want to do something more. What is the next step we can take that will help lay the groundwork for whatever healing ministry might develop?"

A model appropriate for all churches, no matter how extensive or limited their health ministries, is the health cabinet or health committee. The formation of such a group often leads to other developments, such as adding a parish nurse to the church staff. The health cabinet is a tool, a way of involving members of the congregation in a healing ministry to one another. It is based on a wholistic perception of the individual as an integrated organism—body, mind, spirit—each dimension an inextricable part of the whole. We cannot be satisfied with looking only at a person's spiritual or physical health, because each is so bound up with the other that in touching one we affect the whole person.

Individuals also need to be seen within the context of their community—in this case, their families and their churches. As children of God, we are related to one another. It is through community that we derive our support and our encouragement, and this frees us to move toward the health of our whole person.

A. Defining the Health Cabinet

The health cabinet is made up of volunteers who are concerned about health and who are committed to seeing that the healing ministry of the church is carried out. The health cabinet assists individuals and families in becoming more responsible for maintaining and improving their own health and that of their community. The health cabinet is not involved in diagnosis and treatment; that is the domain of the family physician. However, it seeks to be a strong influence on the congregation to the end that stewardship of health is expressed in all areas of church life including worship, education, support networks, and recreation.

The health cabinet works in three main areas:

1. Sponsoring health-related activities through already existing structures and gatherings such as the worship service, Sunday school classes, and youth groups. For instance, a member of the health cabinet might offer to teach a session in various Sunday school classes for different ages on "Your Faith and Your Health." Another alternative is to encourage the book club or library to include books, pamphlets, and audiovisuals on health-related subjects.

2. Sponsoring new programs or activities. If, for example, members of the congregation show a real interest in a particular area of health, members of the cabinet might bring in outside speakers and organize a special event. The health cabinet could sponsor a health fair, devoting a particular Sunday to health issues both during and after the service. The service might include a sermon on the healing elements of faith, contemporary readings on how our faith is related to health, and Bible readings about the healing ministry of Jesus Christ. After the service there might be a series of activities that are typically found at health fairs: blood pressure and cholesterol testing, vision and hearing screening, opportunities to view short films and videotapes, and other activities. This could be followed by a potluck lunch of healthy foods described by the people who brought them. Recipes could be shared.

3. Looking at the overall health and "unhealth" in the life of the whole congregation. If the health cabinet is to have a strong influence on the health of the congregation, this may be the most important of its three areas of activity. Cabinet members work

at ways in which to support health and to turn unhealth around.

One way of supporting health in the church is to
recognize the value of people helping people. Already members express care for one another simply
by listening. Workshops in listening skills can enhance this process and motivate people to listen more
often and more effectively, perhaps even volunteer-
ing to make calls on the sick and listening to them.

A second example is a systematic drawing on the
wealth of members' life experiences by asking everyone to fill out a survey listing areas in which they
might be of help. Almost everyone has been through
experiences—frequently painful ones—that have resulted in personal growth. Even though most of us
are not professional counselors, we have learned
much in certain areas of living that can be shared
with other people. When church members are going
through job change, divorce, illness, or perhaps the
pressures of being a teenager, the health cabinet can
refer them to others in the congregation who can be
supportive. Although these persons may share something of their own experiences, most of all they will
listen.

In these and other ways the health cabinet looks
at ways in which church committees can become
more sensitive to the needs of others. It tries to
encourage people to be more open with each other,
to do more sharing, to be a more healing community.
These are truly major goals of a Christian congregation.

B. The Parish Nurse and the Health Cabinet

The health cabinet is the church committee that
interviews candidates for the position of parish

nurse. Once the nurse is chosen, she becomes a member of the health cabinet. The health cabinet's primary role in relating to the nurse is to provide support. Without such support, the most devoted and talented nurse is likely to experience burnout, followed by guilt for not fulfilling her own expectations. The cabinet members need to support the nurse emotionally, help her decide what needs to be done, assist her with projects, and take on responsibilities delegated to them by the nurse for the healing ministry.

Supporting the nurse comes most naturally to health cabinets that have been in existence for several years. By then they have a good idea of what the healing ministry in their congregation entails and how to go about meeting the needs of people in their church community. When they hire a nurse, or when a nurse volunteers to work with them, they know how to work with her effectively so that all spend their time productively. Sometimes they will work with the parish nurse and sometimes they as the health cabinet will work independently.

When a health cabinet is formed for the purpose of bringing a nurse on staff, it takes a while before the cabinet can act independently. Perhaps they might function well in the interviewing of candidates and recommending to the church council the one who is best qualified. But once the nurse begins her work, they might depend on her to decide what projects to undertake and to organize those projects. At least initially, members of the health cabinet may not feel competent to be in complete charge of a given project. Unless the cabinet is fortunate in having people who immediately grasp the concept of the health ministry and have the vision to give it life, the first months, or even years, may be a struggle. The nurse may find that she has to carry the responsibility alone for a time.

The nurse's job will become easier as the members of the health cabinet begin to see the ways in which they can work alongside the nurse, as well as independently. While the nurse will always put in more time than any other individual, the responsibility for enhancing the health ministry will not rest on her shoulders alone. No doubt she will be energized as individuals take over some of her duties (taking charge of the blood drive, for example), so that she can move on to other projects. And she will benefit from the camaraderie of a team as the health cabinet members put their own ideas into action.

It is vitally important that the nurse has people who are truly working with her—people with whom she can share her excitement in success and her frustrations when impediments keep her from her goal. Such a relationship between the members of the health cabinet and the parish nurse is the key to being an effective support system.

5

What Does a Parish Nurse Do?

It is fascinating to talk with individuals or groups who are hearing about the parish nurse concept for the first time. Invariably, one of their first questions is, "But what do parish nurses do?" And this is often followed by: "Why should the church get into the health business when we already have so many hospitals and doctors' offices to care for our health needs?"

To answer these questions we must remind ourselves that hospitals and doctors' offices are primarily devoted to the care of people after they get sick. Basically, they are sickness institutions. We need them desperately, and we are grateful to live in a country with such an excellent health-care system.

What is sorely lacking in our country, however, is an organized approach to keeping people well. And little by little it is dawning on us that churches throughout the land are places to which millions of people go, week in and week out, to find help for coping with life. Churches, synagogues, and other places of worship should be seen as "health places." People find in these houses of prayer a place where they are helped to rejuvenate their inner selves. And when that happens to the spirit, strength is restored to the physical body as well.

When a Christian congregation decides to have a parish nurse on its staff, either full time or part time, on salary or as a volunteer, new ministries will be inaugurated that will fit naturally into the spirit of a Christ-centered environment.

A. The Parish Nurse as Health Educator

Church members and their friends from the community will be grateful to have the opportunity to participate in well-organized seminars, workshops, Sunday school classes, forums, exercise classes, and small discussion groups covering a wide range of health and wellness topics. The nurse will not do all the teaching or leading. She will bring in qualified people from the disciplines of medicine, public health, social work, nutrition, and psychology, as well as ethics, social justice, and theology.

In some of the congregations we have studied, as many as 300 to 500 different individuals attend one or more such courses or study groups each year. Doctors from the congregations, who have never before been asked to speak about their own specialties, are pleased to participate in this new aspect of church life. It is gratifying to see how many of the speakers seek to relate their Christian faith to the way in which they approach their careers. Many of them have said afterward that this was the first time they had ever given a lecture with a religious dimension. The churches have a serious obligation to stimulate such integration of faith and life.

B. The Parish Nurse as Personal Health Counselor

Parish nurses learn to know the parishioners as they take blood pressure on Sunday morning between services or as they mingle with people in many different settings. Appointments are usually made in an informal manner, with people coming to the nurse and asking, "Could I talk with you sometime?"

To get some perspective on who seeks out the parish nurse and why, we will look at three representative groups:

1. The elderly. Their problems relate to medication, difficulties in communicating with their doctors, and the need for somebody to help them learn to cope with our complicated health-care system. Through personal conversations, the parish nurse is able to assess a parishioner's condition and make appropriate referrals to physicians and other health care professionals. Physicians, in particular, appreciate a parish nurse's ability to discover problems early so that the doctor can be more effective.

2. Parents of preadolescents and teenagers who come with problems concerning drugs, alcohol, and sex.

3. Men over 40. Some of these men took a year or more before they had the courage to seek an appointment with the parish nurse. They always presented a physical problem. This, however, was merely their ticket of admission, because it was apparently all right to go to the nurse for help with

backaches, headaches, or similar complaints. They would discuss their problem for the first ten minutes or so and then go on to talk about how life was treating them, about their worries and anxieties, and about their present outlook on life. When they finally rose to leave, they would say something like, "I've told you things I've never told my doctor. It's easy to talk with you. Thanks a lot!"

C. The Parish Nurse as Teacher of Volunteers

The nurses in our study soon learned that they could not possibly respond to all requests for their help. Gradually they discovered people in the congregation with natural gifts as people helpers. Some had already developed good listening skills through lay ministries groups such as the Stephen Ministries program, which trains people to be one-to-one caregivers in their congregations.

These lay volunteers serve in many capacities. After they have made calls on the sick, they report back to the parish nurse, who becomes their continuing mentor. We assume that soon every congregation with a parish nurse will have a group of well-trained lay visitors whose expertise will increase steadily under the nurse's supervision.

D. The Parish Nurse as Liaison with Community Health Organizations

The United States' complex health care system overwhelms the average person. Parish nurses act as gatekeepers, preventing their parishioners from getting lost in the system. A competent parish nurse has a close working relationship with key people in hospitals, nursing homes, social agencies, and clinics. She knows her way around the field. Parishioners are grateful to her for opening doors to many types of care they had not even known about.

E. The Parish Nurse as Clarifier of the Close Relationship between Faith and Health

Parish nurses have chosen their specialty because the churches provide a unique setting for patients to speak about the deeper things in life that impact on their health. It is a setting in which it is appropriate to talk about doubts and fears of all kinds, including those related to their religious beliefs. In bursts of honesty, parishioners may reveal to the nurse their lack of faith—an admission they may have been unable to make to anyone else.

Many visits to the parish nurse are related to physical symptoms that have developed after the person has gone through a period of loss—perhaps of a job or promised promotion, of friends because of job transfers, or of a spouse or child through divorce or death. It is very likely that their physical complaints are actually grief reactions and may include not only physical symptoms but also a wrestling with ultimate concerns.

Such counseling places a heavy load on the parish nurse, and most nurses will tell you that it takes years of experience and training to help counselees bring the two dimensions, faith and health, into productive dialogue. But most nurses are willing to try, and we believe that God will bless their endeavors.

6

One Nurse's Experience: The First Year

Trinity Church (not the actual name) is a 1,600-member congregation in a Chicago suburb. The church has three full-time ministers. Some years ago the church council agreed to let Trinity be one of the pilot churches for the parish nurse program. The health cabinet was formed immediately as a sub-committee of the congregation's board of Christian education. The cabinet consisted of three doctors, three nurses, a hospital administrator, a homemaker, a university professor, and a businessman. Its first task was to select a nurse to serve on the church staff.

Several candidates for the position were screened by the nursing and pastoral care staff at Lutheran General Hospital. At the health cabinet's second meeting they interviewed the nurses. After group interviews and thoughtful discussions, the health cabinet chose Carol, a member of the congregation who was also on the committee. Although Carol had not originally applied for the position, she was totally committed to the wholeness concept. Carol had a Bachelor of Science in Nursing and credits toward a master's degree in adult education. She had worked for two years as a school nurse, twelve years as a pediatric nurse, and ten years in a women's clinic where she had responsibility for health education.

Carol had lived in the area all of her life except for seven years, and she had attended Trinity since she was a small child. As a result, she had already developed many positive connections with the medical community. The time-consuming task of building initial relationships was behind her. Doctors respected her because they knew that she was, first and foremost, a nurse. People at Trinity had known her for many years. They knew her to be very honest about her own life, and this gave many people the courage to confide in her.

Carol began her work in May. She believed it was a good time of the year to start because it takes about three months to gear up for any kind of program. Since the church slows down its pace in the summer, she was free to prepare for fall activities.

The health cabinet was scheduled to meet with Carol once a month. Carol saw the health cabinet not merely as a board to which she made periodic reports, but as active, hands-on partners in the project. The cabinet members took part in many of the specially planned activities. Programs were not presented by the parish nurse alone but by "the health cabinet and the parish nurse." This partnership brought out hidden talents among the members of the health cabinet. "They were not going to permit shoddy programming," said Carol. "They took their responsibilities seriously."

When Carol joined the staff, considerable attention was given to her new position through the weekly newsletter and the church bulletin. The newsletter became a major vehicle for communication. Each week Carol contributed an article to keep the congregation informed about her work at Trinity and about the role played by a nurse in the context of the church community.

Carol's first major project was to discover the needs of the people in her 1,600-member congregation. She designed a health survey that was distributed at all three Sunday services. The pastor took five minutes during each service to explain the purpose of the survey and gave people ample time to fill it out. It was collected in the offering plate that same day. Because time was provided during the service, there was an unusually good response. The health cabinet studied the results of the survey and then developed programs to fit the specific needs of the congregation.

Carol spent the entire summer laying her groundwork. She chose an office far enough removed from the other church offices to ensure confidentiality, but it was still accessible to the elderly and those using wheelchairs. Since there was no budget beyond her salary, all of her equipment was donated.

Carol spent weeks developing a topical file of health-related materials. She went to local health agencies for information about specific issues. She wrote letters to societies in other places, asking that they mail her information.

Carol visited countless agencies in the community to introduce herself and to learn more about them. Home health agencies, hospitals, senior citizens' centers, and mental health nurses were among her targets. Carol never had trouble getting appointments—even with hospital administrators. She thinks that they were curious about the function of a parish nurse. Home health agencies were grateful to learn that she was not planning to duplicate their services. Through those visits she not only promoted her role, but also was better able to decide whether or not a specific agency was a good referral.

During that first summer, her only health education project was with the vacation Bible school. She offered four topics to the teachers and their classes, and they could choose to attend any two: (1) "How to Brush Your Teeth" (for this she had obtained small tubes of toothpaste from local dentists to give to each child), (2) "Nutrition," (3) "Seat Belts," and (4) "The Big, Bad Cigarette," complete with coloring books.

In September, Carol and the health cabinet began to implement their monthly health education course. Each session was held with the adult forum from eleven to twelve o'clock on Sunday mornings. Announcements of each event were placed in the church newsletter and the Sunday bulletin. The kick-off was a course about how mental stress causes disease. It was taught by a physician who was a professor at the University of Illinois School of Medicine as well as a member of Trinity.

September was also the start-up month of a highly successful weight-loss group that met weekly and of an arrangement for testing blood pressure between Sunday services. Furthermore, Carol had the use of a large bulletin board where she posted timely articles and news of coming events.

However, although Carol became highly visible, there were still relatively few people knocking on her door for personal health counseling. The blood pressure testing provided an opening for some people to talk with her about other problems, but it was still not enough to achieve the necessary break-through. If anything was to happen, Carol needed to take further action.

Every week Carol searched the bulletin for the names of those who were ill or who had been hospitalized. She visited the people in the hospital. If they were part of a family or shared their home with others, Carol called and asked how they were doing and if there was anything she could do. If a husband, for example, had to go to a nursing home, she would go with the wife to help evaluate possible homes suggested by the hospital's social worker. She would make sure that the necessary questions were asked and that they were answered to the wife's satisfaction.

Carol called on a former Trinity organist, a woman in her 80s, and asked for a list of shut-ins who might welcome a visit from the parish nurse. The organist was glad to comply and sent a list of almost 100 names! Overwhelmed but willing, Carol telephoned each person on the list and visited everyone who desired it.

Through such visits Carol became convinced that parish nurses need to be trained in general physical assessment—not a standard feature of nurses' training—because she found that a parish nurse needs to assess individuals' general health in order to determine the correct medical help for them. Carol believes that training in public health nursing is also essential so that when the parish nurse goes into a private home she is able to make the necessary observations about the occupants and surroundings. She needs to know what to say, what not to say, and how to assess the home situation as it applies to mental and physical health.

Gradually people—even adolescents—filtered into the parish nurse's office on their own. They would usually come in with one complaint, perhaps a headache; but as they talked, more problems were uncovered. One teenager came because she was overweight. Carol soon learned that the girl had considerable family stress. Carol invited the parents to come in. They did, and soon she was able to link them up with a family counselor.

Carol was cautious about starting support groups because her schedule was already so full. However, the church did organize a weight-loss support group and an arthritis group. Both meet once a month and bring in a speaker for each meeting.

The organizing of volunteers was postponed until January. Because Carol recognized that she had no training in this area, she went to the local hospital as well as other agencies and talked with directors of volunteers. In essence, she took a tailor-made course in "volunteers." She asked Trinity's former secretary to be the coordinator, because she had the advantage of knowing virtually everyone in the congregation. Together they recruited 50 women who organized themselves as the church's "We Care" committee. These women provide emergency meals, transportation, babysitting, and other services; and they visit the large number of shut-ins among the membership.

To augment her work still further, Carol supervised two nursing students from a nearby college. One of their projects was to put on a mini-health fair on a Sunday morning in January. The congregation was delighted. As usual, there was blood pressure testing. Glaucoma and vision testing was done by a local optometrist. A hospital employee came to measure pulmonary functioning (lung capacity).

Red Cross personnel gave ongoing cardiopulmonary resuscitation (CPR) demonstrations.

After her first year, Carol found that on average she put in a 30-hour week although she was paid for only 20 hours. She derived great satisfaction from her job because she could use all of her talents. She loved working with the members of Trinity and found what seemed to her a series of small accomplishments deeply rewarding. However, Carol has a few words of caution for prospective parish nurses: "The job description is broad," she warns. "Don't try to do everything at once. It will take at least three months just to lay the groundwork, and much longer if you are new to the community." She adds: "A parish nurse must be able to work independently. The rewards will come from the people you minister to."

7

Two Nurses Reflect on Their Ministries

The following conversation provides an intriguing glimpse into the lives, the work, and the perceptions of two parish nurses, Marilyn Belleau, R.N., Glenview Community Church, Glenview, Illinois; and Lois Jean Coldewey, R.N., Lutheran Church of the Atonement, Barrington, Illinois. They permitted the taping of this conversation with Granger Westberg.

Lois Jean Coldewey (LC): The types of problems that people bring to us are chiefly related to health concerns, either their own or those of a family member or friend. But these physical questions usually lead to broader human concerns.

Marilyn Belleau (MB): The first thing that comes to mind in my community is the many problems that middle-aged church members have with their aging parents. They ask if I can get their parents into some kind of home care, day care, or nursing home care. They feel the need to talk at great length about the whole issue. They desire to find some solution to a problem that confronts them day after day.

They usually don't know any professionals in the field, and they need me to refer them to the kind of accommodation that will best fit their relatives' needs. I get a lot of the "What do I do now?" kind of question. It took me months to get in touch with a large variety of agencies, to visit them, and to get a sense of who would feel most at home in a particular setting.

LC: Like Marilyn, I found myself pounding the pavement, visiting all of the neighboring hospitals, clinics, nursing homes, and agencies such as the village hall, the public health department, and the various social service agencies. I would go around ferreting out everything I could find that would help people with literally any kind of problem. And, right from the beginning, we had all kinds of problems presented to us.

A large part of our success in finding answers was due to our networking. We soon got to know scores of people in the helping professions who knew scores of other people like themselves. We keep notes of these conversations and try to learn all we can. All sorts of people become our resources as they share their experiences, good and bad. All of this helps me make better referrals. And this approach is also true of inquiries about physicians. We make a great many referrals to physicians and other health professionals.

MB: I find that calling other parish nurses helps me, even though they may be miles away. I'll ask them what they know about a certain health facility or about some specialist they've worked with. They often give me the name and some data about a person who has special skills in the area I'm concerned about. Then I can help people to move into our complex health system without some of the usual trauma. Once I've been able to help someone in this way, they see me as a friend. And they'll tell their friends. That's why we can't fit all our work into a 20-hour week.

LC: We have wonderful backup from Lutheran General Hospital, which sponsors our parish nurse program. That means ready access to the entire staff of doctors, social workers, psychologists, chaplains, occupational therapists, physical therapists, home health nurses, and all the rest. Often these health professionals will lead an educational seminar on a particular topic in their specialty.

At other times, if a parishioner or a neighbor presents me with a question I can't answer, I say, "I'll consult with a specialist at the hospital." That's very reassuring for them. They know that they will get an expert's opinion. It's an outsider's opinion, which makes it more objective. Then I help interpret that opinion, and they appreciate that we can talk about it in detail, without time or money pressures.

Both nurses agree that most people come to see a parish nurse ostensibly because of physical problems but that this often masks the real reason, perhaps marital discord or something else seemingly unrelated. They have begun to sense a relationship between inner hurts and physical hurts.

The nurses agree, furthermore, that it generally takes people a long time to make connections between their physical health and their faith. Perhaps it begins to dawn on them after attending several church seminars dealing with wholistic health. Gradually they begin to understand that the body often simply reflects the inner turmoil with which they have not yet come to terms. They begin to admit to this turmoil, and later they thank the nurse for taking the time to help them work through their whole problem, not just a piece of it.

LC: Some people open up very quickly, but some don't ever seem to grasp the connection between problems of the body and problems of the soul. Our task as parish nurses is to make that connection real. So I ask in every interview, "What else is going on in your life?" I would not even be able to make a worthwhile referral if I didn't approach the person wholistically. I simply explain that I have to have an overall picture of their lives.

Granger Westberg (GW): Do you think we are being successful in our efforts to help people see their local church as a health-giving place?

LC: It's an ongoing, long-term process, and sometimes it is very frustrating because people think of health as a purely physical concept. As nurses, we have been taught that health is much more than the absence of disease. And now that we work in a Christian church setting, we can discuss the spiritual dimension of health as well.

It often takes a long time to make this much deeper and broader definition of health seem real in a person's life. We have a difficult task before us as we try to educate people about whole-person concepts. To open people up on the subject, I often ask, "Where do you think God is in all of this?" Sometimes this is rather startling to my listeners, but it gives me a chance to put the educational process on a one-to-one basis.

Marilyn and I agree that during our several years of work in a church setting, many things have begun to penetrate the consciousness of our members: Even in conversations during the coffee hour or after church in the narthex, people will say things like, "My back is bothering me again, but I guess it's trying to tell me something. Maybe I'd better talk with you about some things." We believe that these individuals are beginning to make some important connections.

MB: You know, I see the church setting as very conducive to healing. After all, people come to church of their own free will. They are surrounded by people with a common faith in a loving and caring God. They tell me that when they come into my office it is a nonthreatening environment and has nothing to do with money or job security. That is why I think parish nurses have little difficulty in developing good rapport with people. In a subtle way, I think people are reaching out for the basic strengths which the church of Christ has to offer.

LC: But there is still a deep reluctance by most church members to share their brokenness with other members in any kind of group setting. And that disturbs me. What better place than a church for such disclosure? It is rare to hear a person say, "I'm hurting. I lost my job, my husband is working two jobs, I'm lonely, my kids are driving my crazy, I know I'm not being a good parent, I need help!"

Most people in a church setting keep all this to themselves. We give them so little opportunity to find a person or a group with whom they can be totally honest. And yet, how healing that would be! Congregations have the potential to be that kind of health place. I am convinced that in my congregation more and more people are sensing that true health has to do with a person's relationship with God and that their church might just be the place where such a combining of health forces could be brought about.

GW: Please reflect on your ministry in relation to four words: *prayer, forgiveness, self-esteem,* and *addiction.*

Prayer

MB: I am the parish nurse in a huge congregation where no one wants to sound too pious. I find them to be devout people who love the Lord, but they seldom use religious terminology. In private conversations with individuals I find myself just naturally saying, "Have you found help through prayer?" They are almost shocked by such a question. You don't talk about such private things.

I, as a Catholic, grew up with prayers said several times a day. All my friends talked about praying about this or praying about that. It was part of our vocabulary, our way of living. But these dear church members whom I have come to love so much often are hesitant to talk about their prayer life. So we finally got several members to talk out loud about their need to be more open about prayer. We even started two prayer groups that meet regularly and with enthusiasm. Is this what a parish nurse ought to be doing? I think so, at least if we want to be consistent in our understanding of the role played by faith in our total health. I believe there is an openness to turn to prayer these days. I detect an eagerness on the part of intelligent people who live and work in a materialistic world to return to the warmth and power of a meaningful prayer life.

As I seek to deepen my own prayer life, I feel more secure in my role on a church staff—something

I never dreamed of doing! I feel more comfortable discussing prayer with people, and I don't feel I'm encroaching on the clergy's territory, because our church bulletin says, "Every church member is a minister." The response of the people is amazing. I'm glad to be privileged to help people get hold of that side of themselves.

Forgiveness

LC: A powerful word! I think the lack of forgiveness, or lack of being forgiven, is at the root of much disease. That is evident when people present a health problem. Often as we talk with committed church members who have for years been hearing sermons on the forgiving love and grace of God, we discover that they have not accepted this forgiveness for themselves. Nor are they convinced of the strength that would come to them if they would forgive others. They seem unsure that God has forgiven them, and often they carry a terrible burden of hate and resentment toward others.

I think it is essential that parish nurses ask people how they feel about forgiveness. It is a crucial part of keeping them well or making them sick. The fact that the parish nurse places such importance on forgiveness as a part of health care may even stimulate people to rethink certain elements of Christian doctrine as pertinent to their personal outlook.

Self-esteem

MB: I see many people who suffer from a lack of self-esteem. They continually beat themselves over the head. Where I have seen this in its most obvious form is in our support group for those recently divorced. Most of these people are women. For some, their husbands have just walked out on them and left them with small children. Yet these women are saying that it is all their own fault: "If only I had been a better wife." They berate themselves over and over again. They have even taken physical abuse from their husbands and seem to feel they deserved it. That is often their interpretation of being a true Christian!

LC: Lack of self-esteem is a distortion of what our theology is all about. It is ironic, because there are so many people in the church who think they are being called to love their neighbor but not themselves. So when I talk about love of self, or even self-care, it is probably a very foreign concept to them. We need to remember the whole commandment—to love our neighbor as *ourselves!*

Addiction

LC: In the average congregation, addiction is one of the hardest areas to face. No one wants to admit that there are some things that he or she cannot handle. There is a great sense of shame and denial related to addiction—more than any other kind of disease. Appendectomies, gall bladders, even tumors are all right to talk about in public—but not addiction.

In our church we have prepared ourselves to respond to substance abuse problems by training a team of committee lay people to provide information and support. Statistics show that 10 percent of the people in our parishes suffer from the disease of alcoholism. Since the average alcoholic affects four more people, at least 50 percent of us live in close contact with alcoholism. Thank God that the church is beginning to respond to this need for healing, too!

The previous conversations are just a small sample of the subjects that are brought up on a typical day. They do help us realize that the work of a parish nurse is much more than just having a first-aid office in a church building. Of course, as a medical professional, the parish nurse responds immediately to cries for help when someone gets sick or injured, but also of vital importance is her presence as teacher, friend, and spiritual counselor. The work of parish nurses expands our understanding of the potential of any congregation to be a truly healing community.

8

The Parish Nurse: A Bridge between Science and Religion

My years of experience with the parish nurse program have reinforced my conviction that these nurses, through their professional education and in practical experience, have one foot in science and the other in religion. Thus they are ideally equipped for bringing about closer ties between the two disciplines and are already doing so.

Lengthy periods of history have been devoted to antagonism between science and religion. The gap between these disciplines has been very wide. In the health field we have seen this clearly in the uneasy relationship between clergy and physicians. During their college years, future doctors majored in the sciences and had little time left for the humanities. Future clergy, meanwhile, were steeped in languages, history, literature, sociology, philosophy, and psychology. In graduate school medical and theological students saw nothing of each other. They lived in two distinct worlds.

It was only when physicians and clergy began to practice their respective professions that they bumped into each other—at the bedsides of sick people. But even in that setting there was no real communication. Physicians and clergy most often greeted each other and then talked about the weather or sports or community events. This perfunctory relationship is now going through some changes that are long overdue.

Part of the change can be traced back to the observations of hospital nurses who were unusually sensitive to the needs of their patients. They understood that their patients needed more than excellent scientific medical care and often saw to it that their patients received spiritual care as well. But they were bothered by the gulf between physicians and clergy, even though both were ministering to the same patients. Frequently it was at the nurses' urging that physicians and pastors talked with each other about the whole-person needs of patients.

Many of these nurses had entered their profession for spiritual reasons and were uncomfortable with a health care system that did not take into account patients' spiritual needs. It is they who are encouraging a variety of ways in which the large gap between medicine and religion can be closed.

Indeed, patients have appreciated the nurses' interest in this coming together of the two professions. They have felt better when both doctors and clergy have ministered to them. The very word "minister," in fact, defines both professions. When physicians are functioning as whole persons, they are ministering. Patients do not see clergy and doctors as antagonists; they see them as complementing each other in their respective roles. Here are the official representatives of science and religion together in the same room with two very different ways of looking at the world. But to the suffering human in their care, there is every reason for a blending of their resources.

It has been said that science and religion are neither identical nor contradictory. Science alone or religion alone affords but a partial view. We say this now, but we were saying something quite different not so many years ago. Most scientists could not imagine how an intelligent person could fall for the tenets of religion. And many clergy, from their pulpits, were waging warfare against "those atheistic scientists."

What has happened to change these perceptions? Perhaps both groups have grown up a bit. As we have moved toward maturity, we have mellowed to the extent that we are both somewhat more humble about our assessments of each other. A quiet revolution has been taking place in each camp as both religion and science have become aware of the vast areas of exploding knowledge about the universe. Theology has learned from science to become humble in the presence of such magnificent mystery. Scientists, meanwhile, are actually raising moral and theological questions.

Recent breakthroughs in science have affected not only the physical sciences but the biological sciences as well. Physicians know that the old mechanistic theories of biology are gradually giving way to an organismic conception of life, and particularly the life of the human species. Life is now seen to be made of "structural components in a complex and inexhaustible unity." On the one hand, biology is closely related to chemistry and physics. On the other hand, when biology deals with human life, it is related to psychology, sociology, and even philosophy. Then the human has to be seen as a whole—

body and spirit living and interacting in a community of other humans. This wholistic concept envelops mysteries that have not even been plumbed. Yet here, within the context of human biology or the study of the whole person, is a natural place for pastor and physician to meet. Spiritually mature nurses are playing an increasingly significant role as intermediaries in this process.

It is in this modern setting—something that approaches a new compatibility between science and religion—that the parish nurse enters the scene. With an office on the premises of the church itself and with a ministry that is conducted there as well as in homes and hospitals, the parish nurse has a unique opportunity to serve in many capacities. Again we may describe her work as that of intermediary. She helps to create a meeting place for the physical and the spiritual.

The Bible strongly emphasizes the importance of relationships for human health and wholeness. Human beings are never seen as objects. Humans are always described as needing to be in a relationship with both God and other human beings. Science, by its very nature, has always tended to have an "I-it" relationship to whatever is being studied. The scientist in the laboratory observes an object that can be manipulated or measured or weighed. The scientist is the "I" dealing with the "it." And this is quite proper. But when the science is the practice of medicine, the "I-it" approach should be limited to certain areas such as laboratory research.

The moment a relationship develops between doctor and patient, a new dimension is added. Often more significant kinds of healing take place when each honors and respects the other. Doctor and patient are equals in the presence of God, and "gradually the relationship will change from "I-it" to "I-thou.""

Parish nurses seek to bring the "I-thou" dimension to every human contact. Physicians and pastors who have worked with parish nurses have frequently commented on their unusual ability to combine the resources of science and faith.

9

Jesus' Healing Ministry and Our Faith

We cannot think of healing or be a part of it without reflecting upon the Author and Finisher of our healing and our faith. Theologian Krister Stendahl has written, "God's agenda is the mending of creation." Mending is an expression for God's total love toward suffering humanity, of which healing is one aspect. We can say that God's healing light, which was revealed by Jesus Christ, has always been in the world, an indication of God's life-giving and sustaining concern.

Jesus promised that we would do greater works than he did (John 14:12), and it is clear that he demands no slavish repetition, but rather a lively and creative response. Yet there can be no argument that the approach to the healing task, both in spirit and practice, must be drawn from the healing Christ. The rhythm of preaching, teaching, and healing runs all through Christ's ministry. Those who came to him reflected that rhythm, for they came to listen to him and to be healed of their diseases. Again and again we read in the Gospels that Jesus went about "healing every disease and sickness" (Matt. 4:23; 9:35; et al). Jesus accepted people as they were, focused on their individual conditions, and dealt with them. The New Testament makes clear that Jesus' ministry stressed the healing of the whole person. Almost one-fifth of the material in the Gospels is devoted to stories of Christ's healing and the discussions that resulted from them (Morton Kelsey, *Healing and Christianity* [Evanston, Ill.: Harper & Row, 1973], p. 54).

All of life is interrelated and tied to health. An individual human being is an integrated totality of body, mind, and spirit. The health of a human being is affected by the various conditions and influences that are a part of life. Jesus understood this, and in Hebrew culture the body and spirit were not divorced. Jesus viewed the individual as an essential unity, and because of this he was able to envision the essential wholeness of life. Though he was always concerned about healing a person whose body showed signs of physical illness, he rarely stopped there. He paid close attention as well to other manifestations of brokenness in that person's life.

Jesus dealt with the relationships within the person (body, mind, spirit) as well as the relationships between the person and God, the person and neighbor, and the person and the world. These relationships gave a necessary perspective and allowed healing to be approached in a wholistic manner.

Our own experience with relationships and intimacy provides us with evidence that human life is whole, not fragmented. The energy after settling a dispute is more than emotional. The pleasure of sexual intimacy is more than physical. The sharing of common beliefs and prayer in a community of faith is more than spiritual. In human relationships, our entire beings are involved. This is true whether we are hearing of a painful betrayal or sharing an affirmative hug. Relationships are wholistic and therefore a dimension of health.

Today humanity is faced with the question of its own survival on the earth. The term "eco-crisis" has been coined to dramatize this ecological question. Humans are placing a great strain on the earth, and the earth is in pain. With technology as their club, human beings have been beating the earth to death as though it were something to be hated. The earth will tolerate only so much of our human nonsense; after that a process called "dieback" may be triggered. The human species may die back to the point where it barely survives at all.

A. Dust Thou Art, and unto Dust Shalt Thou Return

The biblical basis for stressing our human continuity with the good earth around us is expressed classically in Genesis 3:19: "In the sweat of thy face shalt thou eat bread, till thou return unto the ground; for out of it wast thou taken; for dust thou art, and unto dust shalt thou return" (KJV). The Christian doctrine of creation has tended to neglect the earthly medium of the creation of homo sapiens. Humanity is not external to the earth, but one of its vital forms. The earthly environment gives the human being physical, mental, and spiritual food. There is no direct, unmediated relation between God and humanity in the history of creation and redemption. The earth is always there as a third partner—a creative medium; hence the expression "mother earth." *Adama* is the Hebrew name for earth, whose first son is Adam, the man. The earth is a womb, home, and grave for Adam.

What we believe and how we understand our faith—matters commonly considered to be limited to the spirit or to the mind—actually pervade all aspects of what it means to be human. The person who lives with hope, for example, interprets life differently than one who does not, and therefore feels and acts differently. We have more physical energy, more mental clarity, and more freedom in relationships when we live with a hopeful faith. Conversely, when our outlook on life is informed by guilt, fear, and thoughts of retribution, more stomach acid flows, more fear-related adrenaline is released, and more muscles tense defensively. Faith and healing are interrelated—are inseparable—not only in times of dramatic healing but each day of our "healthy" lives.

Experiences we consider to be purely emotional also involve our whole selves. Consider the relief that often follows crying. We take a deep breath, clear our thoughts, and get on with our lives, feeling a little more whole than before. Laughter often functions in the same way, renewing our perspective and liberating us physically. Mental health professionals are discovering what we have always experienced: anxiety, depression, and other problems involve our whole person, including our relationships, our faith, our physical state, and even our eating habits.

Mark 2:1-12 illustrates that Jesus' healing was not confined to either the physical or the spiritual realm.

When a paralytic was brought to Jesus, he said simply, "Your sins are forgiven" (v. 5). In so doing, he went beyond the paralytic's external ills to the man's deeper needs. The man took up his pallet and walked because Jesus understood that the body and the spirit are a unity.

From the Scriptures we know that Jesus sent his disciples out to continue his ministry. He told them to preach the kingdom of God and heal the sick. It may be assumed from the manner in which Jesus approached his healing ministry that he intended to heal the whole person. We read in the Book of Acts how the church sought to carry out this commission—caring for whole persons, not souls or bodies alone. These early Christians were inspired by a sense of wholeness in their mission to the world. They believed that the new quality of life that Christ came to impart was to extend to the entire human being: body, mind, and spirit. Thus from the outset, healing was considered an integral part of the church's ministry.

A word that aptly describes health is *enabler*. Good health, understood wholisticly to include body, mind, and spirit, enables us to act on the possibilities that are open to us. As Christians, we are called to take good care of ourselves and also to relate to others in ways that help them be whole and healthy.

When health is viewed wholisticly, the picture we conjure up in our minds of a "healthy" person is changed. We all know people who, despite handicapping conditions, lead very full and healthy lives. Some have reached a state of inner wholeness through physical illness. Their illness enabled them to wrestle with their faith and to reach a deeper sense of wholeness in spite of a broken physical body. We also know people who look physically healthy and seem to have everything going for them, yet their lives appear to be empty. People who do not take advantage of the health they have are inhibiting their involvement in the process of living and creating.

From a biblical perspective, healing is a part of the process of living. Health is ongoing; it is not a state that is reached because there are no symptoms of disease. With this in mind, it seems apparent that healing is an activity that is not reserved strictly for the sick. "Healthy" people need care, too. Healing needs to be an everyday occurrence.

10

Whole Person and Whole Earth

Carl E. Braaten

[This provocative article was written by an eminent Christian theologian, Professor Carl E. Braaten. It is a radical expression of why the Christian church ought to take health and preventive medicine more seriously.]

The Meek Shall Inherit the Earth

Humanity and earth exist together in a mutually dependent relationship. A person cannot be whole without a whole earth. When the earth becomes sick, people become sick. Human beings are part of that earth, and the earth is part of human beings.

Little light on the subject of the health of the earth and of human beings can be found in the great biblical and systematic theologies of recent times. Christian theology has dealt mostly with the salvation drama—creation and fall, sin and guilt, cross and resurrection, the church and the last things.

The question of the health of the body and of the earth has rarely been posed. But in the biblical vision salvation is no partial process that concerns merely a part of the totality of reality, the part called the "soul." The biblical vision is all-embracing; the earth goes together with heaven and the body goes together with the soul. Salvation includes health and healing.

When we moderns destroy the balance of nature, not only are soil, plants, and animals affected, but the human body also pays a price. The earth lashes back, and the harmony between earth and humanity is destroyed.

Would we continue to plunder our environment if we saw ourselves as bodies in natural continuity with the earth? "No one ever hated his own body, but he feeds and cares for it" (Eph. 5:29). If the body is seen as the very stuff of the earth, then such a thing as soil erosion will not be viewed with indifference, but as a serious disease of the body. Similarly, the spreading of the human species on the earth beyond the capacity of this small planet to provide each member a full measure of healthful food will be regarded as a terminal illness, as fatal as a cancer growing in the body. An infinitely expanding Gross National Product can be seen as another form of cancer in the whole body of humanity and earth.

What we must hope for is a new attitude to the physical world, consisting of a profound respect for the delicate connections between all creatures and a mystical harmony with the earth as the source and ground of our bodily life. Albert Schweitzer's philosophy of reverence for life must be commended in spite of the fact that it was nourished by Eastern mysticism rather than by Christianity.

Western philosophy has inherited a prejudice against nature. It has been predominantly a philosophy of ideas (Plato) or of consciousness (Descartes) and more recently of existence (Heidegger) or of language (Wittgenstein), but the bodily basis of thought is not reflected in any of these great systems.

My investigations have not reached a point where I can explain why Christianity has retained so little of the "somatic" in its spirituality and theology. It has excelled in its stress on individuality and personality, forgetting that it is the body that individuates the personality. Where would I be without my body? The I-Thou relationship is a pure abstraction without the flesh and blood that bump against each other.

Christianity veered into spiritualism as it accommodated to the Greek world. At the same time it mishandled its Jewish sources. It is hard to deny that dominant trends in Christianity have simultaneously nourished supernatural and antinatural attitudes, driving humanity into an egoistic subjectivism and reducing nature to a mechanism subject to humanity's brutal will.

The body-soul dichotomy reflects itself in a split between human beings and nature, between the subjective spirituality of humanity and objective world.

The Israel of the Old Testament tended to split the world into two realms, opting for the God of history against the God of nature. The struggle between Baal and Yahweh was a struggle between the god of fertility and God of history. What Israel achieved was to make the god of fertility subject to Yahweh, the Lord of history, so that Israel was liberated from the worship of earth, from cultic participation in the rituals of earth's renewal. But this liberation did not mean that, in entering history, she abandoned nature. Israel did not expel the mysteries of fertility, did not sever her connection with the earth. The promises she lived from include hope for a good land flowing with milk and honey.

The rectification of an unbalanced attitude toward the earth in Christian spirituality will require us to be more radical in our approach to the Old Testament.

We will have to look at the creation hymns and at the hymns of judgment. In Psalm 104, for example, the poet depicts the world—vegetable, animal, and human—as God's creation. God's breath is the life principle of all things. The hymns of judgment arise in face of the evil deeds of humankind. People damage and destroy the creation of God, including themselves. They do not care for the earth, so the earth mourns and languishes by the violence of people (Hos. 4:3). Heaven and earth witness against them; they have the people's oaths of allegiance to the Creator but have suffered the full force of their violence. If we read the Old Testament with eyes renewed by ecological sensitivity, we will see things to which we were blind before. Israel's vision of humanity and its earthly environment can inspire in us a new wisdom of the beauty of the earth made whole, a vision in which union with God includes humanity's commonality with the whole creation.

Physician, Heal Thyself

The chief dynamics of American society cause illness and bad health. The modern practice of medicine is almost entirely symptomatic; it treats symptoms, relieves pain, but neglects the whole person and the conditions of living that excellent health presupposes.

Americans are not healthier than they used to be. The standard of living has been rising since World War II, but the quality of life has been declining. The growth of technology has given us false trust that things are getting better. To be sure, technology has given us new techniques in sanitation, antiseptics, and surgery. And, indeed, many conspicuous diseases have been conquered—diphtheria, polio, tuberculosis. But the degenerative diseases have been quietly galloping into epidemic proportions.

Millions of Americans suffer from heart disease; they speak of their high blood pressure, arteriosclerosis, angina. Millions suffer from diabetes or hypoglycemia, both connected with the fact that after World War II the consumption of sugar in America rose dramatically. Two disorders directly linked to nutrition are constipation and insomnia.

The concept of the whole person within the whole context of life is blatantly disregarded.

A culture can hardly be called a culture when it rears its youth in almost total ignorance about the fundamental arts of life: farming, cooking, eating, working, playing, exercising, meditating, fasting, praying, and making love.

My judgments have been short and snappy. They are intended, however, to provoke us to more reading and reflection. If they can be supported, and I think they can, then they roll themselves into this one question: What must we do to be saved?

I want to emphasize that Christianity ought to reclaim its message of healing. The Christian message is the healing of the whole person, or it is a false religion.

RESOURCES

A. Whole Person Health Inventory

When a nurse talks with people about their health, the word *health* takes on a broader and a deeper significance than usual. To discuss the health of a human being means more than just a description of bodily functions.

For years spiritually minded nurses have wished that there might be ways to assist people who are healthy as well as those who are unhealthy to take a closer look at more of the factors that are customarily observed in a "physical checkup." The idea of a parish nurse inviting people to sit down with her to discuss health topics grew naturally out of the experiences these nurses have had with their parishioners.

The Whole Person Health Inventory is designed to help bring about more thorough and wide-ranging conversations with parishioners about the interconnectedness of body, mind, and spirit. Most checkups neglect to take seriously a person's outlook on life, almost as if it does not matter. One's philosophy of life, or faith stance, is at the center of one's being. Therefore, it plays an important role either in keeping one well or in making one sick. Effective health care dare not neglect it.

Our world is tremendously influenced by scientific ways of approaching all aspects of life. We are greatly indebted to the scientific method, and we reap all kinds of benefits from it—especially in the area of health care. But science limits itself to the nonreligious areas of living. Scientific textbooks do not speak of God because they are not dealing with the spiritual realm. Science deals with material things, and we are grateful for its magnificent discoveries. Yet, because so much of our time is spent dealing with material things, we don't find it necessary even to mention how our belief in God affects us.

Belief or disbelief in God does affect us! That is what we are learning from contemporary studies that are probing into what make us sick and what keeps us well.

Our scientific mindset makes it difficult for us to speak openly about mystery. We feel uncomfortable about revealing our thoughts concerning prayer or worship. A discussion with the parish nurse who has one foot in the sciences and one foot in the humanities makes it easier for a person to talk about all the factors that are part of either sickness or health.

For many people God exists as an idea, a vague hope, a name chanted to, but not as a tangible presence. To a large degree, we have lost our sense of the sacred. We seldom talk about sacred things apart from sermons in churches. That does not mean that people do not have spiritual experiences. They do, but usually they keep quiet about them lest they be thought strange. This inventory makes it possible for people to speak honestly and openly about great moments in their lives. They are also free to speak about the darker moments when they have felt separated from God.

Where do people have opportunities to speak confidently with a caring Christian person? Most people rarely find themselves in settings where such in-depth explorations are possible. We have discovered that such honesty concerning matters of the heart and the struggles of life is often part of a discussion about health problems. It is an ideal setting for such interaction. The nurse admits her own need for spiritual help and shares her insight, and soon the parishioner feels free to describe personal experiences with spiritual dimensions.

In such conversations, the parish nurse is engaged in a ministry of healing as she helps people realize the presence of God in our lives—a realization that gives life its meaning, focus, and direction. A ministry of healing is a "standing alongside" those who are in pain.

Whole Person Health Inventory

One's body, mind, and spirit are interdependent. Good health care involves the whole person. One's outlook on life is a primary ingredient in maintaining one's health. This inventory can assist you in reflecting on your wellness in a wholistic manner. After you have completed this inventory, you may, if you wish, ask your parish nurse for time to discuss it.

A. THIS SECTION CONCERNS CHANGES IN YOUR LIFE.

1. Life changes often create stress and may affect your health. Please check such events that have occurred in your life the past year or two. Star those that have been most stressful to you.

_____ Death of a spouse
_____ Death of a family member or close friend
_____ Divorce
_____ Personal illness
_____ Difficulties at work
_____ Marriage in the family
_____ Change in health of family member
_____ Outstanding achievement (graduation, promotion, etc.)
_____ Change in degree of self-confidence
_____ Change in church activities
_____ Change in work responsibilities
_____ Change in relationship to parents
_____ Change in drinking _____ smoking _____ drug use _____
_____ Change in residence
_____ Change in financial condition
_____ Change in spiritual life and practices

2. We all cope with stressful change in different ways. Please check the various ways in which you respond.
    a. Cry _____ Eat _____ Take long walks _____
Meditate _____ Talk it out _____ Go shopping _____
Drink _____ Become irritable _____ Feel guilty _____

Pray _____ Blow my top _____ Clean house _____
Blame others _____ Listen to music _____ Find a good
book _____ Bottle it up _____ Headaches _____ Stomach-
aches _____ Tense muscles _____ Other _____

b. I find quiet time for myself:
frequently _____ occasionally _____ never _____

c. I have one or more friends or family members in
whom I can confide about personal matters.
Yes _____ Did have _____ Not now _____ Seeking _____

B. THIS SECTION CONCERNS YOUR RELATIONSHIP TO GOD.

1. What word or image best describes God to you?
_____

2. When you have gone through difficult times in the
past, has your relationship with God been helpful to you?
Usually _____ Somewhat _____ Never _____
Please explain. _____

3. At the present time, how do you feel about your
relationship with God?
Feel good _____ Mostly feel good _____ Not pleased
with it _____ Seldom think about it _____

4. Do you think your relationship with God has anything to do with the quality of your life?
Yes _____ No _____ Explain. _____
_____

5. Do you believe there are aspects of one's religious
belief or church life that could make one ill? Explain.
_____

6. What people in your life had the most to do with
forming your current opinions about religion? Describe.
_____

In what ways was God important to your mother?
_____

Your father? _____
Your guardian, if not brought up by parents?
_____

7. Do you belong to groups that discuss such matters as ethics, values, and religion? I have in the past _____ Never _____ I belong to such a group now _____ I would like to belong _____. Do you find such discussions helpful? Yes _____ No _____ Please comment. _____

8. Have you had a life/religious experience that has influenced you? Yes _____ No _____. If yes, please describe. _____

9. Do you have a favorite Bible story? _____ A favorite Bible character? _____ What makes them special? _____

10. What church activities help make your life more spiritually meaningful? Worship services _____ Bible studies _____ Other educational programs _____ Small groups _____ Personal conversations _____ Music groups such as choir _____ Seminars _____ Service and outreach programs _____ Other _____

11. What three things do you wish God would grant you?

    a. _____
    b. _____
    c. _____

C. THIS SECTION CONCERNS YOUR RELATIONSHIP TO YOURSELF AND OTHERS.

1. Are you involved in the care of another person? Yes _____ No _____ If yes, describe. _____

2. Are you satisfied with your immediate family relationships? Yes _____ No _____

3. Do you have a physician who knows you? Very well _____ Fairly well _____ Hardly knows me _____

4. When did you last have an appointment with a physician? This past year _____ Two or three years ago _____ Four or more years ago _____

5. How recently have you had a complete physical checkup? _____

6. Are you taking any medication? Yes ____
No ____. If yes, for what purpose? _____

7. How many days were you ill during the past twelve months? About ____ days. Type of illness: _____

8. How would you evaluate your present health?
Excellent ____ Good ____ Fairly good ____ Not too good ____

9. Are you concerned about good nutrition? Eat anything ____Watch my diet ____ Health nut ____

10. How many times each week do you eat the following: Eggs ____ Meat ____ Poultry ____ Cheese ____
Low-fat milk ____ Whole milk ____ Cream ____
Vegetables ____ Fruit ____ Hamburgers ____ White bread ____ Desserts ____ Salads ____ Whole grain bread ____ Whole grain cereals ____ Salty foods and snacks ____

11. How often do you drink alcohol? Daily ____
Almost daily ____ Occasionally ____ Never ____

12. Is anyone concerned about your drinking?
Yes ____ No ____

13. Is anyone concerned about your medication or drugs?
Yes ____ No ____ Yes, in the past, but not now ____

14. Do you smoke? Yes ____ No ____. If yes, what, and how many per day? _____

15. Do you exercise? Yes ____ No ____. If yes, what kind of exercise? _____. How often? _____

16. Are you at your ideal weight?
Above ____ Below ____ About right ____

17. How is your blood pressure?
Normal ____ Above ____ Below ____

18. How is your cholesterol?
Normal ____ Above ____ Below ____

19. Do you use car seat belts?
Always ____ Sometimes ____ Never ____

20. In general, how do you feel about your life and your health at the present time? _____.
Name (Optional) _____.

B. Characteristics and Qualifications of a Parish Nurse

The following is based on the description from Iowa Lutheran Hospital's Minister of Health Education Program. Similar outlines have been used by other hospitals, church agencies, and congregations.

Education

- Be a registered professional nurse with a current nursing license.
- Have a B.S.N. or R.N. with active participation in continuing education programs related to parish nurse responsibilities.

Experience

- Two years of previous nursing experience.
- Experience in any of the following is beneficial: public health, education, nursing homes or care centers, physician's office, school nurse in public schools, medical-surgical nurse, emergency-outpatient nurse.

Personal

- Knowledge of the health/healing ministry of the church.
- Knowledge and practice of wholistic health philosophy.
- Sensitivity to integrating and applying the spiritual aspects of wholistic health personally and professionally.
- Skill in communication and teaching/learning techniques.
- Knowledge of health services and resources in the community, including public health and hospice.
- Motivation to grow personally and professionally.
- Knowledge of current nursing and health care issues.

- Participation in church and community activities that contribute to professional growth and to the promotion of wholistic health philosophy.
- Knowledge of and compliance with the Code of Ethics of Nursing and your state's nurse practice act.
- Practice of confidentiality and professional standards.
- Membership in professional organizations encouraged.

C. Sample Job Description of Parish Nurse as Minister of Health*

Summary

The minister of health provides wholistic health care (mind, body, and spirit) for individuals, families, groups, the congregation as a whole, and some aspects of the community; utilizes quality communication skills with clients; collaborates with pastors, parish staff, and community resource personnel; promotes comprehensive health care; brings assertive approach to wellness; and assumes an accountable role.

I. Responsibilities and Duties

A. Promotion of health care delivery for parishioner(s)/congregation(s).
  1. Collects health pattern data to identify complex health care needs.
  2. Organizes and analyzes complex health pattern data to develop needs strategies.
  3. Establishes goals with the parishioner(s) to develop a comprehensive approach to health care needs.
  4. Evaluates the health care delivery system and promotes goal-directed change to meet the health care needs of parishioner(s)/congregation(s).
  5. Acts as advocate for parishioners on health-related issues/problems.

---

*From Iowa Lutheran Hospital's Minister of Health Education Program.

B. Promotion of spirituality—Educates parishioners to maximize healing resources of the church
   1. Worship
   2. Sacraments
   3. Education
   4. Fellowship
   5. Service and outreach
   6. Wherever healing grace is experienced
C. Communication with others
   1. Utilizes complex communication skills in interviewing and counseling individuals, families, and small groups.
   2. Develops and maintains goal-directed interactions to promote effective coping behaviors and to facilitate change in behavior.
   3. Designs and implements health care teaching plans within the congregation. Provides formal/informal teaching for individual families with special health care concerns.
D. Advocacy/communication on behalf of others
   1. Initiates and facilitates referrals to appropriate community health care resources.
   2. Promotes the development of new/existing resources that meet spiritual health-related congregational/community needs.
   3. Coordinates the delivery of health care services and recommends changes in health care delivery.
E. Management of health care
   1. Assumes a leadership role in improving health care delivery with the congregation/community.
   2. Documents and communicates data to provide continuity of care and services.
   3. Maintains accountability for own care and care delegated to others to ensure adherence to ethical and legal standards.

II. Qualifications

A. Graduate of a state approved school of nursing
B. Current licensure as a registered nurse (in state of practice)

C. Two years of previous nursing experience

D. Completion of a clinical pastoral education/minister of health education program, Iowa Lutheran Hospital

D. Sample Role Description of Parish Nurse as Minister of Health*

The following list is an overview of health ministry possibilities in a congregational setting and elaborates on the activities mentioned in the job description:

A parish nurse or minister of health:

1. Is a person who is an experienced registered nurse with spiritual maturity and a commitment to healing ministries.
2. Functions as a member of the pastoral team serving the congregation, neighborhood, and community by bringing an assertive approach to wellness, wholeness, and prevention.
3. Brings wholeness and healing to God's people in specific ways by functioning not primarily in the medical model, but in the pastoral model of caring.
4. In the pastoral model seeks to minister with and beyond the realm of medical technology and its systems in order to assist the church to fulfill its role in the healing of all aspects of creation.
5. Embodies by design and function a vital theology of the body to enable specific care and service for the whole person in body, mind, and spirit.
6. Is not to be seen as a primary health care giver, but one who facilitates use of available resources of a community and church.
7. Seeks to maximize the healing heritage that we have in the Christian tradition in our worship, sacraments, outreach, support groups, educational groups, service groups, koinonia—whereby we experience grace that is healing.

---

*From Iowa Lutheran Hospital's Minister of Health Education Program.

8. Is an educator, advocating consumer information by enabling people to know what health services are available, how they may be used, whom to contact, and what the costs are. This is done in a pastoral model with home visits that allow assessments so that early intervention can be made.

9. Addresses from a spiritual perspective the life-style issues that face our society, and seeks creative ways to enable people to find more healthy and realistic patterns for living and dying.

10. Is a catalytic networker and coordinator of community services within the pastoral role, assisting a person or family in a continuous manner through many different systems, institutions, and agencies until the necessary care and service is obtained or created.

11. Is an innovator and assists congregations and community groups in discovering and creating new approaches to changing societal needs, to enable a more abundant life for all God's people.

12. Has appropriate gifts, knowledge, expertise, and abilities in the disciplines of pastoral care, community nursing, social work, wholistic health, wellness, and personal growth.

E. What a Parish Nurse Might Request

The following is adapted from *Nurses in Churches: A Manual for Developing Parish Nurse Services and Networks* by Jan Striepe. The manual is available from National Parish Nurse Resource Center (address on page 140).

Jan Striepe, parish nurse at Trinity Lutheran Church in Spencer, Iowa, drew up a paper for the church council that included her goals and requests.

These were her goals:
- To develop an organized health ministry
- To teach health and wellness to individuals or groups
- To evaluate whether a parish nurse can be effective in assisting members to adopt healthy life-style habits, and
- To promote a wholistic health philosophy.

She drew up this list of requests and clarifications.

Liability insurance. (Jan's own professional liability insurance was current. The church's insurance agent checked the church's liability policy and communicated that there was no problem in having a parish nurse program at Trinity.)

Salary. (She requested to be an unsalaried employee of the church.)

Budget. (She requested a budget allotment of $1000 to be used for health education, continuing education, some equipment, and needed texts.)

Hours. (Her hours as parish nurse were Tuesday mornings from 9:00–11:00. Also, members could call her at home.)

Fees. (She charged no fees because the parish nurse was a ministry of the church.)

Office space. (She requested the resource room as the parish nurse office.)

Phone. (She asked that an extension phone be placed in the resource room using the same number as Trinity's preschool.)

Secretarial time and copying. (She said she would need secretarial assistance occasionally, not to exceed six hours per month, and use of the copying machine, not to exceed 100 copies per month.)

Accountability. (She and the pastor planned to meet at least every other Monday. The church council would receive written reports monthly. In addition, she would communicate and coordinate her work with the Christian education and social ministry committees. She asked that the church pursue the goal of establishing a health committee in the future to assist her in implementing and evaluating aspects of the church's health ministry, as well as providing a support group for her.)

F. Models and Types of Parish Nurse Services

If a nurse or church is considering implementing a parish nurse service, it is helpful to evaluate what type or model would be best for the situation. As the parish nurse concept has evolved, many different models have developed.

I. Parish Based

A parish nurse service without a formal relationship with other parish nurses or local health or social agencies, or other social agencies or facilities. The service may or may not have an informal relationship with other agencies or facilities.

A. Advantages
  1. Less time involved in planning, since only the church council and its committees are involved.
  2. More autonomy, because the parish nurse would not be required to have the approval of a hospital or health agencies for implementation of health programs.

B. Disadvantages
  1. Less communication and networking between the parish nurse with health providers in the community.
  2. Possibility of lack of access to health education pamphlets and resource people.
  3. Lack of consultation and sharing with other nurses.

II. Parish Nurse Service with Relationship to Hospitals

Parish nurses are initially salaried by the hospital for a specific length of time, such as eight hours per week for a year. The church agrees to salary the nurse after the initial start-up salary provision.

A. The hospital's contributions
   1. It could provide health education pamphlets.
   2. It could make available support and resource persons (chaplains, a discharge planning nurse, social workers, others).
   3. It could assist with the parish nurse orientation curriculum.
   4. It would have Continuing Education Unit (CEU) programs applicable to the parish nurse's role and responsibilities.
   5. If the hospital has a hospice program, the parish nurse could assist in recruiting and support lay hospice volunteers from the church or could serve as a hospice volunteer.

B. The parish nurse's contributions
   1. She could provide a communication link between the discharge planning nurse and parishioners who have been hospitalized.
   2. She could provide enhancement for the hospital's public relations.
   3. She could disseminate hospital health education pamphlets.
   4. Because a parish nurse would be knowledgeable about wholistic health, she could assist in hospital programs to promote wholistic health life-styles of hospital employees.
   5. Because one of the roles of parish nurses is to serve as a referral person, the nurse would educate and reinforce the importance of annual physical exams by physicians as well as encouraging prompt visits to physicians when symptoms are present.
   6. Establishment of guidelines, organized curriculum, and so forth would be more thorough if there were an established relationship among parish nurses, a hospital, physicians, and social workers.

III. Parish Nurse Service with Relationship to Community Health

A. Public health's contributions
   1. It could provide health education pamphlets.
   2. It could make available support and resource persons.
   3. It could possibly assist with the parish nurse orientation curriculum.
B. The parish nurse's contributions
   1. She could help with health promotion. A concept that could be considered would be the following: If the public health office would establish a contract with the parish nurse(s), the activities of parish nurse(s) such as health promotion programs, blood pressure screening, and visits could be included in the public health monthly statistics. There could be a network of RNs working in health promotion, and the public health department could certainly increase its health promotion activities.
C. Other advantages
   1. Referrals could be made to and from community health nurses.
   2. Establishment of guidelines will be more thorough if there is an established relationship between parish nurses and community health nurses.
   3. If there is a formal or informal relationship, misunderstanding and duplication of services can be avoided. By the existence of effective communication, health services will be enhanced by parish nurses.

IV. Other Models

A. Parish nurse service and area agency on aging
B. Parish nurse service and a wholistic health center
C. Parish nurse service and colleges

D. Parish nurse service and nursing homes

E. Parish nurse service and social agencies

F. Parish nurse service and colleges of nursing

G. Coalition model (cooperation of churches, hospital, social agency, and others to implement a parish nurse service and network)

This list was adapted from *Nurses in Churches: A Manual for Developing Parish Nurse Services and Networks* by Jan Striepe. Available from National Parish Nurse Resource Center (address on page 140).

G. Minister of Health Education Program

Iowa Lutheran Hospital in Des Moines has developed a well-planned education program for registered nurses who are interested in becoming ministers of health in congregations. The following draft from Chaplain David Carlson tells the story and provides an overview of the program.

Goal

The goal of the minister of health education program is to prepare professional registered nurses to serve in a parish nurse role within congregations and communities and to apply nursing and pastoral knowledge for health promotion, intervention, and health education in all areas of life of those persons served by the church.

Objectives

The overall objectives undertaken in this program focus on development of relationships and structures that will enable the identification, exploration, and testing of various aspects of this new opportunity in ministry. Specifically, there were three major objectives pursued in the first phase that was funded by grants for three years: (1) to graduate six professional nurses through a year-long program of internship, (2) to create and test a model of education and curriculum content that provides the appropriate professional development, and (3) to work with congregations and their denominational structures to explore the feasibility for further financial support and development within the established church structures.

A Brief History

Early in 1983 a consultation was held between James Anderson, administrator of Iowa Lutheran Hospital; Rev. Jerry Schmalenberger, pastor of St. John's Lutheran Church; and Rev. David Carlson, director of pastoral services at Iowa Lutheran Hospital. The purpose of the exploration was to discover ways in which a hospital and congregations could seek to foster better health care for people in the congregations and the communities by utilizing the resources of both the health care systems and the churches. Reverend Schmalenberger, in his ministry, found it very helpful in specific situations to ask for the assistance of a registered nurse who could help to assess individual and family situations and provide appropriate information referrals and use of resources to meet the need.

Out of this conversation, David Carlson wrote a proposal that explored the establishment of a year-long internship experience that would be modeled on an extended unit of Clinical Pastoral Education because he is a certified supervisor with the Association for Clinical Pastoral Education. That paper was used as a stimulus to talk to hospital administrators, congregational pastors, nurses, and other interested professionals to explore and expand the ideas and the concepts and to help envision future possible developments.

In March 1985 a 12-member task force was selected to pursue the development of this program. Membership on this task force consisted of six nurses involved in clinical nursing and nursing education; representatives of parish clergy, medicine, social services, and chaplaincy; and hospital administrators. For the next year and a half this task force applied itself to the study and research necessary for the development of this program. The task force diligently studied the interest of churches and nurses, the expectations of the role, entrance requirements, curriculum and training experiences, resources that were needed to establish the program, and ways to prepare congregations for the use of the new role as well as marketing of the program.

To facilitate their work, the task force members studied papers written by persons prominent in developing the minister of health concept and consulted with church officials, nurses, nursing educators, and congregational pastors to obtain appropriate feedback. Subcommittees were organized to prepare documents outlining the curriculum design and content, funding sources and budget, job descriptions, and the relationship of the minister of health position to the church structure.

An important key to the development of the minister of health role is the education and information sharing with congregations and their clergy. The questionnaire developed by this task force and distributed to all denominations throughout Iowa showed that 76 percent of the clergy felt a minister of health would be utilized either frequently or occasionally by members of their congregations, especially in the areas of personal health counseling, health education, visiting the sick, and making health referrals. The questionnaire distributed to nurses identified their needs and concerns and showed that a primary component of the curriculum needed to be appropriate pastoral theology and pastoral care orientation and education. This need as articulated by the prospective nurses provided the impetus to the development of a curriculum that has a strong pastoral theology content. The conclusion now, after three years, from those nurses who are in the role of the minister of health, is that this is the foundation upon which this role is built and is vital to the growth and development of the ministry within the congregation.

The task force continued by hiring a grant writer to propose and write grants that would fund this three-year test phase. With the securing of grant monies, the program was able to proceed by engaging congregations and nurses in this exploration without being hindered by limitation of finances. This enabled congregations to explore the possibilities with minimal investments and to take over more of the financial responsibility as the credibility of the ministry grew within the congregation through its own experience and practice. This has proven to be a very effective way to test and demonstrate the possibilities for ministry within a congregation and to document the validity of this role and the necessity for congregational financial support as well as for denominational support.

The first class of seven registered nurses began their year of internship in the fall of 1986. The program attracted nurses and congregations from all over Iowa. Some of them committed to commute 180 miles one way in order to participate in the program. In the first three years of this program, 1986 to 1989, 27 congregations were involved in supporting this ministry and receiving the services of a minister of health. There have been 8 Lutheran, 8 Roman Catholic and 8 Methodist congregations, 1 congregation each of Presbyterian, Christian (Disciples), and Friends (Quaker). In three of these settings, one nurse has served two or more congregations; this has provided new understandings of the ways in which this role can be utilized and multiplied and has also provided opportunities for congregations to move into this new ministry without the total financial responsibility resting on a single congregation.

Methodology

Nurses and congregations apply for admission to the program separately or together. A two-stage interview process is used for interested nurses who submit an application with the appropriate materials and are interviewed and qualified as appropriate for admission to the education program. Following this, they are recommended to interested congregations as potential candidates, are interviewed and evaluated by the congregation for appropriateness, and may then be employed by the congregations. When employed, a nurse may enter the year-long internship and engage in ministry development within a congregation.

The first three weeks of the year are a time of intensive orientation and education. The major focus within this framework is the experience within the Clinical Pastoral Education program at Iowa Lutheran Hospital to study and practice appropriate pastoral theology and pastoral care concepts. During this time, the nurses function as chaplains within the Pastoral Services Department and learn to integrate their own spiritual and theological understandings into their nursing perspective. The second major focus of this initial phase is the integration of wholistic concepts within this role. Drawing on the resources from theological scholarship and nursing practice, the nurses explore their own understanding and move toward the integration and appropriation of a pastoral nursing style appropriate to each individual.

An identified need in this period of time is the development of a collegial community that provides the ongoing nurture, support, and professional resources that are essential for this ministry within the congregation. Through this time, the nurses come to know each other individually and professionally and learn to trust and respect each other; this experience provides a powerful foundation for continuity as the nurses venture into new dynamics and experiences within their own congregational settings. It affords the appropriate affirmation, collegial support, and professional challenge that are necessary in this pioneering venture.

The program curriculum covers the following areas: pastoral care, wholistic health and wellness, community health nursing, and community resources (see pages 113-115). The total curriculum time is approximately 250 hours. The first 120 hours are covered in the first three weeks of full-time involvement. During the next three months, the nurses return to the hospital for one and one-half days every two weeks. In the following remaining eight months, the nurses return for one-day sessions each month. A special graduation ceremony is held at the end of the year-long program.

Following the initial three-week period, the nurses undertake a more regular schedule at their internship sites.

The list of actual activities and projects undertaken by the nurses in the minister of health role is very comprehensive (see pages 116-118 for examples).

Throughout the internship experience, the nurses are under the direction of a supervising pastor and advisory committee or health cabinet and the director of the minister of health program. Each congregation is required to establish a health cabinet or similar resource group as a part of this program. This committee, the congregation, and the pastoral staff determine the focus and the ministry content for each specific congregation. They also work toward the clarification of specific job descriptions that are appropriate to the ministry and mission of that setting. The nurses work with members of their congregation in fulfilling this ministry and engaging those members in ministry to one another. The nurses then return periodically to the hospital for the classes, collegial sharing, fellowship, and resource exchange.

Evaluation Processes

Evaluation processes have been built into the plans in order to continue the development and refinement of this educational program.

1. Nurses provide ongoing oral feedback regarding the curriculum and their internship experience during the scheduled seminars. This aspect is established early in the program as it is an integral part of the Clinical Pastoral Education model.

2. During the year, written evaluations are given to the program directors by the nurses, the supervising pastors and other pastoral staff, advisory or health cabinet committee members, and congregational members.

3. At the end of the year, written evaluations and perspectives are given by the nurses and others involved in the program as listed above.

4. The progress of the nurses in meeting the objectives of the curriculum are determined through the seminar

discussions, the portfolio evaluations, and personal conferences with the supervising pastors and the program director. In some congregations, the advisory committee also provides evaluation input.

Significant Developments

From the very outset, the issue of entrance qualifications has been discussed. This program has been designed specifically for registered nurses and is envisioned to continue with this basic premise. We feel that it is necessary to maintain consistency as we attempt to build a solid foundation for this ministry's educational program. We hope that out of this experience we will not only know more clearly the requirements necessary for registered nurses in this new role, but also will be able to design specific educational curriculums for other nurses and human services professionals. As this new ministry grows and as the networks develop for professional exchange, we are already seeing the development of specific models that will address these professional needs.

The experience in this program has developed the term "pastoral nurse," although "parish nurse" is also a valid title. This term documents the new understanding that is essential to a minister of health role. The existence of such a role is not merely an extension of the medical or nursing model into the congregational scene. This is a new application of the historic role of the deacon or deaconess and represents the current integration of the theological and nursing professions appropriate for this day.

This role functions on the premise of what is called "the pastoral prerogative." Within our religious setting, pastors are still given the prerogative to initiate interventions and to seek to establish a helping or serving relationship by their own initiative. By combining the nursing role with the pastoral prerogative, we have maximized the benefits of two disciplines in a way that can effectively and efficiently minister to the wholistic health needs of people within our congregations and communities.

The success of this new ministry within any congregation is highly dependent on the actual relationship between the supervising pastor and the minister of health. Intentional time and energy must be spent on the development, clarification, and nurturing of a positive, open, interactive, professional relationship in order for the nurse to be integrated into the whole life of the congregation. The nurse will meet regularly with the pastoral staff as a group and individually with the supervising pastor for specific consultation. To efficiently facilitate a good collegial relationship, we found helpful the establishment of a suggested format to assist the pastor and nurse to clarify their relationship (see pages 119-120).

Included in our development process has been the articulation of a generic job description (see pages 93-95) and a role description for the minister of health (see pages 96-97). A congregation can use the generic job description as a guideline to develop a specific job description appropriate for their setting. The role description of the minister of health is a helpful tool in educating a congregation and its clergy regarding the overall perspectives essential to the development of this ministry.

One benefit of the consistent evaluation and feedback mechanisms that are essential to this program has been the ability to monitor the variety of activities, functions, and ministries that have been developed in congregations through the presence of the minister of health. Monitoring provides a comprehensive view of what is possible within a congregational setting through the initiation and facilitation of the minister of health program.

Each year's class of nurses is invited to reflect and assist in further development of proposed standards of care for a minister of health. While we have had only three years to refine these standards of care, we hope that eventually this effort will be the foundation upon which this new role will be acknowledged as a specialty within the nursing profession and that this role will find acceptance within nursing guidelines and legislation (see pages

121-124). Much more development needs to be experienced, reflected upon, and documented in order for this hope to be realized.

Note: Copies of questionnaires, feedback forms, and other instruments may be requested from Chaplain David F. Carlson, Iowa Lutheran Hospital, University at Penn Avenue, Des Moines, IA 50316.

1) Curriculum Design and Content*

I. Design

The curriculum design is patterned after a Clinical Pastoral Education program. The year-long program begins with an intensive three-week session that provides the nurse with a foundation to move into an internship setting in a church. During the next three months, the nurses return to the hospital for one and one-half days every two weeks. In the following eight months, the nurses return for one-day sessions each month.

Structured seminars held at periodic intervals will facilitate integration of concepts from various content areas with experiences from the nurse's internship and will allow sharing of these experiences and ideas with other nurse interns.

The nurse intern will be expected to make a full commitment to the program for optimal learning to occur.

A certificate will be awarded to the nurse intern upon completion.

II. Content

Specific curriculum content is developed in each of the areas listed. The nurse intern is responsible for documenting how each of these competencies has been achieved during the internship experience.

A. Pastoral care
   1. Clinical Pastoral Education
   2. Orientation to the minister of health role and responsibilities
   3. Ethics and ethical decision-making
   4. Death and dying, loss and grief ministry

---

*Developed for Iowa Lutheran Hospital's Minister of Health Education Program.

    5. Prayer, sacraments, and healing services
    6. Pastoral theology
    7. Pastoral ministry
    8. Witnessing and sharing your faith
    9. Communication skills and verbatims
   10. Dynamics of working on the pastoral team and understanding church structuring

B. Wholistic health and wellness
    1. Concepts of wholistic health and wellness (mind, body, and spirit)
    2. Meaning of illness
    3. Stress and stress management
    4. Self-care
    5. Risk factor reduction, sampling classes, and screenings
    6. Wholistic health community resources
    7. Sexuality throughout the life cycle

C. Community health nursing
    1. Standards of care
    2. Legal implications of nursing practice
    3. Health assessment tools
    4. Education program planning and teaching skills

D. Psychosocial concepts
    1. Crisis intervention
    2. Chemical abuse
    3. Child and adult protection
    4. Eating disorders
    5. Suicide
    6. AIDS
    7. Disabilities
    8. Advocacy
    9. Family assessments therapy and support
   10. Counseling theory and techniques
   11. Social service system
   12. Geriatrics and needs of special age groups
   13. Support groups
   14. Behavior modification
   15. Community resources and referral system

E. Other
   1. Assertiveness training
   2. Marketing the minister of health concept
   3. Working with volunteers

III. Prerequisite

A. Graduate of a state-approved school of nursing
B. Current licensure as a registered nurse (in state of practice)
C. Two years of previous nursing experience

IV. Educational resources

A. For seminars:
   1. Iowa Lutheran Hospital: Clinical Pastoral Education Program, Department of Patient and Family Services, Combined Interests Department, Nursing Practice, Public Relations Department
   2. Grand View College
   3. Drake University
   4. University of Iowa
   5. Lutheran Social Services
   6. Ministers of Health
B. For internships/clinical experience:
   1. Iowa Lutheran Hospital
   2. Churches

2) What a Ministry of Health May Include*

A Listing of Health Ministry Activities, 1986–88

1. Wholistic Health Educator

Wellness weekend—health fair
Vial of life, Blood pressure
Knowing your prescription
Cardiopulminary resuscitation
Update your first-aid kit
Conflict management
Sabbath-keeping
Life stress
Corporate wellness
Meditation/relaxation
Sexuality/sex education
Dying, death, grief, and loss
Lifeline emergency phone system
Do you have a living will?
Newspaper, TV interviews
Wellness for youth
Parenting
Bioethics
Life-style change
The caring question
Healthy refreshments for meetings
Living with PMS
Time management
Violence in the home
Chemical health

Gifts of the Spirit workshop
Grief clinic
Good touch—bad touch
Healthy heart
Prayer, stress, and healing
The homeless and the church
Good nutrition
Caring for elderly parents
A spiritual Christmas
Prayer and meditation
Cancer treatment
Mental health and depression
Unplug the Christmas machine
Life-style wellness changes
Free to be thin
Health and the Bible
Chemical dependency
Drugs and intervention
Living with Alzheimer's disease
Spiritual disciplines
How to ask your doctor questions
Women's/men's health issues
Eating disorders
Retirement planning
Seminar on aging

---

*From Iowa Lutheran Hospital's Minister of Health Education Program.

2. Personal Health Consultant

Personal health assessments
Blood pressure screening
Diabetes screening
Cholesterol screening
When to call the doctor
Gifts and self-esteem
Ministry to pastors and staff
Personal prayer requests—
staff meetings
Spiritual support group
Case conference with
pastoral staff
Medical release forms for
church trips
First-aid kits in church and
vehicles
Health and safety in the
nursery
Fire/smoke alarm check—
church and homes
Blood and organ donations
Neighborhood ministry
outreach
Resource for street people
Building accessibility
Temple talks, children's
sermons
Sermons, meditations,
homilies
Expanding the prayers of the
church
Services of prayer and
healing

Worship/devotions in nursing
homes
Staff education, consultation,
and listening
Planning your own funeral
Advocate for nursing home
patients
Church as a nonsmoking
facility
Marriage enrichment retreat
Glaucoma screening
Cards/calls of concern
Personal/family crisis
intervention
Resource file and referral
information
Medical service for
uninsured
Transitions from home to
nursing home
Ministry to homeless
Resources for people of
special need

3. Advocate for Healing Ministries

Home visits
Pre- and post-hospital visits
Nursing home visits
Expectant new mother visits
Dysfunctional family visits
Senior center establishment
Volunteer network for home care
Widows' support group
Unemployed support group
Living with chronic illness group
Caregivers' support group
Mothers' day out
Well-baby clinic
Nursery attendant training
Clown ministry
Utilizing nursing home care review process
Phone ministry follow-up
Coordinate transportation pool
Establish and train for prayer chains
Developing member referral network
Confronting child and family abuse
Shepherding program
Fellowship hall walkers' group
Low-impact aerobics
Stop-smoking clinic
Weight loss support group
Happy birthday call/card/visit
Parents of teen support group
Parents anonymous group
Child sexual abuse education

AIDS support group
Sickle Cell support group
Meals and fellowship for seniors
Refugee family health needs
Shelter ministry for abused
Children's ministry to/with elderly
Caring community training
Partners in health (one-to-one)
Stephen Ministry training
Well-adult screening clinic
Rent-a-kid
Befrienders training
Training for greeters
Quilting group at shut-ins' homes
Adopt-a-grandparent
Divorce support group
Arthritis support group
Adopt-a-student (college and elderly)
Alzheimer's caregiver support group
Christmas tree (gifts)
Cards in narthex ("prayer for")
Eucharistic ministers' training
Home health care coordination
Retreat for the elderly
Hunger hike promotion
Single parent support group
Babysitting training class
Health standards for day care program
Telephone "buddy" network

3) Staff Relationships of Pastor and Minister of Health*

Pastors and nurses may use this outline to facilitate good collegial relationships and to clarify their expectations.

1. What are our role definitions and expectations?
   - I see my role as . . . and your role as. . . .
   - What I hope to be able to be/do in this role myself and with you is. . . .
2. Ways we can share this ministry:
   - For me spiritual disciplines and devotions are. . . .
   - I experience collegial support when. . . .
   - The comfort limit between personal and professional for me is. . . .
   - I handle issues of confidentiality by. . . .
3. Now, because we want to communicate . . .
   - When do we meet? By appointment? Whenever? "Catch me if you can"?
   - My style of communication is characterized by humor, analysis, brooding, etc. . . .
   - What is easiest/hardest for me to talk about is burdens, joys, needs, etc. . . .
   - The way I give/receive feedback and/or criticism is. . . .
4. Our teamwork style probably will be characterized by . . .
   - Dependent/independent/interdependent functioning as when. . . .
   - Initiatives and creativity, for example. . . .
   - Expressions of permission, approval, empowerment, as when. . . .

---

*From Iowa Lutheran Hospital's Minister of Health Education Program.

5. In the day-to-day responsibilities of reporting and accountability . . .
   - The actual reports we need are. . . .
   - The important functions/events to attend are. . . .
   - The space/time available in the bulletin and newsletter will be. . . .
   - The hours of work/time off/schedules issues are. . . .
   - The office space/use of secretary/access to information issues are. . . .
6. In this new venture together, when all else fails, we will. . . .

4) Standards of Care*

The minister of health uses the nursing process to promote wholistic health care in all areas of life to those persons served by the church.

Standard I: Assessment

The minister of health systematically and continuously collects data about the health status of the parishioner(s) and congregation(s). The data is accessible, communicated, and recorded.

Criteria

1. Collects health pattern data to identify actual and potential health problems and limitations. Assessment includes physical, emotional, and spiritual aspects of health.
2. Utilizes individual, family, church, and community resources in the data collection process.
3. Researches the existing health care delivery system.
4. Maintains confidentiality and respect for individuality.
5. Analyzes and interprets data and determines nursing diagnoses.
6. Facilitates individuals to assess their own health status.

Standard II: Planning

The minister of health establishes goals with the parishioners, church staff, and the health advisory committee to develop a comprehensive approach to health care needs.

---

*From Iowa Lutheran Hospital's Minister of Health Education Program. This section is a preliminary draft and is not final. As of publication, the standards are being further developed and refined.

Criteria

1. Integrates wholistic health care into the church's total program.
2. Collaborates with other health care providers, professionals, and community resource personnel.
3. Directs goals toward regaining or maintaining a maximum state of physical, mental, and spiritual health.

Standard III: Intervention

The minister of health intervenes to promote, maintain, or restore health, to prevent illness, to effect rehabilitation, and to assist individuals to cope with alterations in life-style and the effects of loss.

Criteria

1. Reflects God's love through professional and personal caring behaviors.
2. Promotes goal-directed change in life-style to meet the health care needs of parishioner(s) and congregation(s).
3. Acts as an advocate for parishioners on consumer health rights.
4. Assists with visitation in hospitals, nursing homes, homes, and other areas where ministry is needed.
5. Facilitates the use of community resources and makes appropriate referrals.
6. Serves as a resource for health information.
7. Enables, supports, and encourages congregational participation in church ministries.
8. Provides health counseling.
9. Promotes health education for all age groups in the church.
10. Encourages health screening and disease detection practices.
11. Educates parishioners to maximize healing resources of the church. This includes worship, sacraments, liturgy, fellowship, education, service, and outreach.

12. Promotes spiritually based values in decision-making processes.
13. Promotes the development of new and existing resources that meet spiritual health-related community and congregational needs.
14. Coordinates the delivery of health care services and recommends changes in health care delivery.
15. Documents and communicates data to provide continuity of care and service.

Standard IV: Evaluation

The minister of health evaluates the response of the individual, congregation, and community to interventions to determine progress toward goal achievement and to revise the plan as indicated.

Criteria

1. Assesses changes in parishioner(s) and congregation(s) with regard to health care needs.
2. Meets with pastors, parish staff, and representatives of the congregation(s) to evaluate the impact of the health ministry and coordinate program planning.
3. Sets priorities that contribute to the church's total ministry and long-range goals.

Standard V: Quality Assurance and Professional Development

The minister of health is committed to standards of excellence in nursing practice, assumes responsibility for professional and personal development, and contributes to the professional and personal growth of those assisting in health ministry.

Criteria

1. Establishes a mechanism for self-evaluation and evaluation by parish staff and parishioners.

2. Incorporates changes in practice suggested by evaluation.
3. Maintains accountability for own care and care delegated to others to ensure adherence to ethical and legal standards.
4. Assumes a leadership role in improving health care delivery with the congregation and community.
5. Participates in continuing education activities to maintain license and increase knowledge and skills.
6. Participates in professional and community organizations.

References for Standards of Care

Available from Iowa Lutheran Hospital (address on page 140).

- American Holistic Nurses Association Standards of Care
- American Nurses' Association Standards of Gerontological Nursing Practice
- Specific Standards of Care and Patients' Rights for Home Care Patients
- Standards of Community Health Nursing Practice
- Minister of Health Education Program Job Description
- Health Ministry Objectives by Carol Smucker, R.N., M.A.

H. Parish Nurse Agreement between Lutheran General Hospital and Congregations

THIS AGREEMENT is entered into this _____ day of _____, 19 _____ between _____ hereinafter referred to as "Parish" and LUTHERAN GENERAL HOSPITAL, INC., d/b/a Lutheran General Hospital—Park Ridge, an Illinois not-for-profit corporation, hereinafter referred to as "LGH."

WITNESSETH

WHEREAS, LGH and Parish desire to enter into an agreement whereby LGH will provide a Parish Nurse to Parish on a part-time basis;

WHEREAS, LGH provides health care services which include the services of professional nurses;

WHEREAS, Parish is a church seeking to meet the needs of its congregation and to fulfill its spiritual commitment, which includes assisting with physical, emotional, and spiritual aspects of health care;

NOW, THEREFORE, in consideration of the mutual covenants, obligations, and agreements set forth herein, the parties agree as follows:

DEFINITIONS:

PROJECT. The term *Project* refers to the plan by which LGH and the Parish shall place a nurse on the staff of the Parish to provide certain health care services.

PARISH NURSE. The term *Parish Nurse* refers to the registered nurse providing health care services to the Parish/congregation. The Parish Nurse shall be an employee of LGH and shall be under the exclusive control and direction of LGH with respect to all professional nursing services and related activities of the Parish Nurse to be provided through the Project.

I. TERM

1.1 This Agreement shall be effective on the date hereof and shall remain in full force and effect for an initial term of one (1) year. Thereafter, this Agreement shall be automatically extended for successive one (1)-year periods unless terminated as hereinafter set forth. All terms and provisions of the Agreement shall continue in full force and effect during the extension period(s), except those contained in Article IV, which shall be subject to modification by mutual agreement.

II. TERMINATION

2.1 Either party may terminate this Agreement at any time, with or without cause, upon sixty (60) days prior written notice to the other party.

III. OBLIGATIONS OF THE PARTIES

3.1 LGH agrees:
   a) To provide, in conjunction with the Parish as set forth under the terms of this Agreement, a Parish Nurse on a part-time basis, or greater than forty (40) but less than eighty (80) hours per two-week pay period, whose work shall be performed in accordance with the job description attached hereto and incorporated herein as Exhibit A. Should the Parish desire the services of the Parish Nurse on a full-time basis, or greater than eighty (80) hours per two-week pay period, the parties agree that appropriate adjustments shall be made to the Parish

Nurse's salary and that the Parish shall pay the full amount of any salary increase. Any adjustments to fringe benefits shall be negotiated with the Hospital and provided by the Hospital in accordance with Section 4.1(a)(iv);

b) To obtain appropriate verification of the credentials and licensure of all Parish Nurses providing services under this Agreement;

c) To sponsor continuing education to Parish Nurses as needed;

d) To maintain to provide proof to the Parish of professional liability insurance coverage in the amount of One Million Dollars ($1,000,000.00) per claim made with respect to the actions of Parish Nurses who are LGH personnel;

e) To provide salary and benefits to Parish Nurses who are LGH personnel, which shall include all those supplemental benefits offered by LGH to hospital-based part-time employees; and

f) To reimburse the Parish Nurse for travel expenses to meetings and continuing educational programs at LGH in accord with LGH policy.

3.2 Parish agrees:

a) To provide the facilities, furnishings, educational materials, and equipment as may be required at the Parish by the Parish Nurse;

b) To form a Health Committee in the Parish to assist the Steering Committee, as hereinafter defined in Section 5.3, in coordinating the work of the Parish Nurse;

c) To provide secretarial support from the Parish's secretarial office as may be required by the Parish Nurse;

d) To encourage and facilitate the active participation of the Parish Nurse in continuing education of the Parish Nurse sponsored by LGH; and

e) To reimburse the Parish Nurse for the travel expenses of the Parish Nurse within the Parish community in accord with Parish policy.

IV. COMPENSATION

4.1 Payment

(a) Parish shall reimburse LGH for a portion of the yearly salary of the Parish Nurse in the amounts set forth below:

    i. The first year: Parish shall pay LGH twenty-five percent (25%) of the nurse's yearly salary as determined by LGH, in consultation with the Parish, for the Parish Nurse's services, payable in three (3) installments at approximately four-month intervals on dates to be determined by LGH;

    ii. The second year: Parish will pay LGH fifty percent (50%) of the nurse's yearly salary as determined by LGH, in consultation with the Parish, for the Parish Nurse's services, payable in installments as set forth in (i) above;

    iii. The third year: Parish will pay LGH seventy-five percent (75%) of the nurse's salary as determined by LGH, in consultation with the Parish, for the Parish Nurse's services, payable in installments as set forth in (i) above; and

    iv. By the fourth year, and for each year thereafter, the parties agree that the parish will pay to LGH the full amount of the Parish Nurse's salary, as determined by the Parish, in consultation with LGH, and LGH will continue to pay the fringe benefits and malpractice insurance, and provide overall supervision, continued education, and quality control of the program.

(b) Salary Adjustments

    i. LGH will periodically provide the Parish with data on comparable nursing salary ranges in the Chicagoland area, and the parties mutually agree to use these salary ranges as a basis for establishing the Parish Nurse salary;

ii. Parish will conduct an annual performance appraisal of the Parish Nurse, using performance appraisal forms supplied by LGH, and shall consult with LGH in the performance appraisal of the Parish Nurse; and

iii. Parish shall make appropriate adjustments in the Parish Nurse salary at the time of each annual performance appraisal, in consultation with LGH, based upon the salary ranges provided and the performance appraisal conducted in accord with this Section 4.b.ii.

V. GENERAL COVENANTS AND CONDITIONS

5.1 Records

All records created and maintained by the Parish Nurse shall be the property of LGH. These records shall be considered confidential. LGH and Parish agree to comply with applicable LGH policies and procedures and all applicable state and federal laws, rules, and regulations governing the release of these records.

5.2 Personnel Policies

The Parish Nurse, as an LGH employee, shall be subject to LGH personnel policies regarding his or her employment.

5.3 Steering Committee

A Steering Committee shall oversee the Project and assure its mission, quality, and effectiveness by performing the following functions:

a) To maintain liaison among LGH, Project staff, the Parish Nurse, the Health Committee, and the Parish to assure that the Project is operational;

b) To assess the Project's value, consistency with concept, effectiveness, and future growth to make those changes deemed necessary for a fuller implementation;

c) to develop means and resources to establish, evaluate, maintain, and measure the Parish Nurse's unique role as health educator and counselor;

d) The membership of the Steering Committee may include but shall not be limited to:

    i. Chairman of LGH Pastoral Care or designee;

    ii. Vice President of LGH Nursing Service or designee;

    iii. Primary care physician designated by LGH;

    iv. LGH Administrator or designee;

    v. Legal Counsel designated by LGH;

    vi. Project Director designated by LGH;

    vii. Parish Pastor or designee; and

e) It is mutually agreed that the Parish, through its pastor and/or designee, will attend and participate in the meetings and activities of the Steering Committee.

5.4 Selection of Parish Nurse

Both parties shall participate in the selection of the Parish Nurse. LGH shall consult with the Parish in the selection of the Parish Nurse, but the determination of the professional competence of the person or persons selected shall be made exclusively by LGH. The parties agree that all candidates must be approved by both LGH and the Parish; final selection of the Parish Nurse from the approved candidates shall be made by the Parish.

5.5 Termination of Parish Nurse

Should the service of a Parish Nurse terminate or be terminated, a new Parish Nurse shall be hired in accordance with the process established in Article III.

5.6 Indemnification

The parties agree to indemnify and hold each other harmless from any liability claim, demand, judgment, and costs (including reasonable attorneys' fees) arising out of or in connection with the intentional or negligent acts of their respective employees and/or agents.

5.7 Compliance with Laws

The parties shall comply with the requirements of all county, municipal, state, federal and other applicable governmental authorities, now in force or which may hereafter be in force pertaining to the performance of this Agreement, and shall faithfully observe all municipal and county ordinances, state and federal statutes now in force or which may hereafter be in force.

5.8 Independent Contractor

Nothing contained in this Agreement shall constitute or be construed to create a partnership, joint venture, employment, or agency relationship between the parties and/or their respective successors and assigns, it being mutually understood and agreed that the parties shall provide the services and fulfill the obligations hereunder as independent contractors, and the Parish Nurse shall not be deemed to be an employee or agent of the Parish. Further, it is mutually understood and agreed that nothing in this Agreement shall in any way affect the independent operation of either LGH or the Parish. The governing body of LGH and the Parish shall have exclusive control of the management, assets, and affairs at their respective institutions. No party by virtue of this Agreement shall assume any liability for any debts or obligations of a financial or legal nature incurred by the other.

5.9 Notice

All notices required to be served by provisions of this Agreement may be served on any of the parties hereto personally or may be served by sending a letter duly addressed by certified or registered mail. Notices to be served on LGH shall be served at or mailed to: 1775 West Dempster Street, Park Ridge, Illinois 60068, Attention: Chairman, Division of Pastoral Care, with a copy to _____, 1775 West Dempster Street, Park Ridge, Illinois 60068, unless otherwise instructed. Notice to be served on Parish shall be serviced at or mailed to _____ unless otherwise instructed.

5.10 Inclusion of All Terms and Conditions in Writing

This Agreement embodies the whole agreement of the parties. There are no promises, terms, conditions or obligations other than those contained herein; and this Agreement shall supersede all previous communications, representations, or agreements, either verbal or written, between the parties hereto.

5.11 Written Modifications

The Agreement may be modified at any time in writing by mutual agreement of the parties.

Lutheran General Hospital, Inc.
d/b/a Lutheran General Hospital—Park Ridge
An Illinois Not-for-Profit Corporation

By: _____

Parish:

By: _____

PAA/jab
5548G/VS
041888

I. A Rural Parish Nurse Network

After I had begun a parish nurse service in 1985 at Trinity Lutheran Church (350 members) in Spencer, Iowa, I was certain that I was not unique. I thought other nurses would become parish nurses and volunteer their time if there was support, educational opportunities, and some tangible incentives such as resource books, pamphlets, and an educational stipend. Also, I felt that parish nurses could be valuable health resources in small congregations in rural areas. Thus began my journey as a parish nurse coordinator.

Before attempting to initiate a rural parish nurse network, I looked at characteristics of our rural area. The population of 16,000 in Clay County, Iowa, is dispersed, with one town of 11,000 and ten other towns averaging less than 400 people each, with the farm population making up the rest. Another significant fact was that nearly 17 percent of the area's total population was 65 years old or older.

The data about hospitals, churches, and the economy were also pertinent. All of the hospitals in a 60-mile radius are small (ranging from 20 to 100 beds), and many of them were struggling financially. Most of the hospitals' governing bodies were city or county and therefore did not have an affiliation with a church denomination. The churches in the area ranged from very small (less than 200 members) to very large (more than 1,500 members), most of them in the 300- to 400-member category. The economy of northwest Iowa was very depressed, since farming is the backbone of the economy and the farm crisis was in full force.

Several other factors were noted. None of the small towns had a physician; many nurses were working part-time; many nurses were already using their nursing skills and knowledge within their church and community and, in effect, functioning as "informal parish nurses."

Since a hospital-based parish nurse network was not feasible, Greg Anliker, director of the Northwest Aging Association, assisted in obtaining a grant from the Northwest Area Foundation in St. Paul. The one-year project's goal, which began in September 1986, was to establish an ecumenical network of ten parish nurse programs in a nine-county area. The parish nurses emphasized health promotion and health maintenance of the elderly.

The project's components include:

Parish nurse: A registered nurse (RN) functioning as a wholistic health educator, resource person, and referral person in a church setting.

R.N.s selected for the program would receive:
- $500 stipend for attending educational sessions
- Resource books and pamphlets
- CEU certified educational sessions (approximately 50 hours)
- Assistance from a parish nurse coordinator

R.N.s would agree to:
- Attend the educational sessions
- Volunteer approximately four hours per week
- Maintain data about clients and activities

Churches would agree to:
- Support and encourage the parish nurse service
- Provide office space, phone, and office supplies
- Consider future funding of the parish nurse service through salary and/or expense reimbursement

The project was very successful. A summary of that beginning year includes some interesting statistics. There were twelve parish nurses in the nine-county area. Partial data about their activities include 2,052 client visits at the church; 379 home visits; 85 health promotion presentations; and 273 referrals to physicians or health or social agencies. In addition, they wrote health articles in the church newsletters, maintained bulletin board displays, and even organized health fairs.

Numbers are important. However, the people that the parish nurses assisted tell the real story. Here are a few examples.

An elderly woman was in need of home health assistance, but she refused to allow the community health nurse and nurse aide to assist her since she thought their services were "welfare." The parish nurse visited her at home and was warmly received because the woman knew she was from her church. By the end of the visit, the woman had agreed to assistance from community health and said she would welcome visitors from their church.

Another nurse initiated "We Care" volunteers to assist church members with needs. Several nurses initiated exercise classes at their churches, including exercises for seniors; the fellowship was as important as the exercise! In one small town (pop. 800) with seven churches, the parish nurse began having monthly health presentations at her church. People from all denominations attended those programs. Grief support groups were very helpful since the small towns had not had them before.

There were many instances where the parish nurses responded to members' crisis situations by arranging for other members to assist and by contacting health/social agencies. For instance, they have assisted elderly persons' placement in nursing homes. The rapport of the pastor and the nurse with the elderly person eased that difficult decision and transition. This is especially important because many times the elderly person did not have children living in the community.

Some elderly persons living on a fixed income who would qualify for programs such as fuel assistance did not seek assistance, but instead stopped buying their medications in order to pay their utility bills. A nurse assisted by educating and supporting those persons in completing the forms or by referring them to the elderly advocate of the Aging Association.

The health program topics that nurses have spoken on or arranged speakers for have been diverse. Some examples include healthy snacks (taught at vacation Bible school); farm safety; pesticides; caring for the care-giver of a spouse or elderly parents; parenting; and, of course, wholistic health.

Some examples of a lack of understanding about the parish nurse role are worth noting. At first, members and even pastors tended to focus on "hands-on" nursing tasks and illness-oriented aspects. Some members wanted the nurse to perform venipunctures for insurance requirements, and one wanted the parish nurse rather than the public health nurse to change a catheter. One pastor asked the nurse to obtain and give the necessary immunizations for the youth group to attend Bible camp. The nurses declined such requests, explained why, and referred those making requests to the appropriate person or agency.

The nurses met every month for sharing of ideas and support in 1988, but this decreased to every other month in 1989. The nurses' work schedules make it difficult for them to meet. Communication is maintained by telephone and a regular letter describing their activities and "news."

Of the twelve volunteer parish nurses who began, eleven are still in the program. Three have received a salary; one of the three has an interesting "salary." At her church, on the first Sunday of the month, a basket is placed in the narthex with a poster stating "Donations for the parish nurse." Other churches have had bake sales and rummage sales to give the nurse money for needed equipment and supplies. One nurse is reimbursed for her expenses such as long-distance phone calls.

The eight nurses not receiving a salary have not pursued seeking a salary. The majority of them simply said that this was something they wanted to do or that the money simply was not available because of tight church budgets. Another comment from a nurse was that she is doing her parish nursing instead of teaching Sunday school. It should be noted that all of the rural parish nurses except one work full-time or part-time elsewhere in nursing and do not want to work more hours as a parish nurse. Also, the majority are in congregations of fewer than 500 members and are able to affect members' lives by working four hours a week. In comparison to the above example, a nurse would need to work 20 hours in a congregation of 2000 to serve a comparable number of members.

None of the congregations have established a special health committee. Instead the nurses work with and through the social ministry and Christian education committees. At my church we have changed the social ministry committee to the social and health ministry committee.

By describing the ecumenical parish nurse service in rural northwest Iowa, I hope several aspects are evident. First, it is important to assess what model of parish nursing is workable. Certainly I wish all parish nurses were salaried; however, that is a barrier in the rural area. A specific description may help. A 250-member church with 40 percent elderly members, many on fixed incomes, relies heavily on people giving of their time and talents. Janitors, choir directors, church treasurers, and others are not paid for their services. Another aspect is the difficulty of obtaining start-up money for a paid coordinator, CEU sessions, stipend money, and resources for the nurses.

Second, the description of the nurses' activities illustrates that the services they offer are similar to those of their urban counterparts, simply because human needs are similar wherever people live. Sometimes the rural area is thought of as peaceful and serene with fewer problems than urban areas. In reality, the rural areas have as many stressors as urban areas. However, because the volunteer nurses have narrower perimeters of activities because of the time constraint, it is important that other members of the congregation are utilized in enhancing and developing health and healing programs. As volunteers, the nurses need support and guidance to avoid burnout as well as to help in prioritizing their activities. Thus, a buddy system or a coordinator who can provide support and educational direction is important.

There are also advantages for the parish nurse project in rural areas. The most obvious one is that many nurses were already doing "informal parish nursing" in their church and communities. Another advantage is that, in small towns, the church and church activities often have an important influence on individuals and the community. Also, the nurses in the project had the trust and acceptance of members because the members had known the nurses for years.

I would like to close by sharing an experience I had. One day I visited a delightful elderly widow who is a member of our congregation and who has had intermittent bouts with various illnesses including hypertension. When I checked her blood pressure, I obtained very high readings. I called her physician's nurse, relaying the blood pressure readings, and was instructed to bring her to the office.

The physician was very pleasant and thorough during the exam and interview. After giving her instructions on a new medication and other aspects of her illness, he turned to me and asked, "Could you check her blood pressure tomorrow?" When I said, "Yes," he paused and then asked, "You're a public health nurse?" I replied, "No, I'm a parish nurse." He said, not unkindly, but matter-of-factly, "Oh, then you have no official capacity."

The physician immediately turned and began to speak to my elderly friend, so I just smiled and did not reply to his comment.

However, I wasn't smiling that evening when I relayed the event to my husband. Actually, I was angry. After verbalizing for about five minutes, I disgustedly said, "I guess I have to be part of some health care delivery system in order to be 'official'."

My husband, who is a hospital administrator and familiar with health care acronyms such as PPOs and HMOs, paused a moment and then quipped, "Next time, just say you're with the OHO, the Original Health Organization!"

That event reminds me that the church is the OHO whether the church is in a rural or urban area. It also reminds me that new programs take time to develop, and during that development time, it is important to explore many different models. Parish nurses functioning in different models still have the same end result. They respond to the health needs of their church members and community and provide a valuable addition to the ministry of the church.

J. Addresses

Chaplain David F. Carlson
Iowa Lutheran Hospital
University at Penn Avenue
Des Moines, IA 50316
(515) 263-5154

National Parish Nurse Resource Center
Lutheran General Hospital
1775 West Dempster Street
Park Ridge, IL 60068
(708) 696-8773